CREATING
COMMUNION

CREATING COMMUNION

The Theology of the Constitutions of the Church

John J. Markey, O.P.

Foreword by
Thomas F. O'Meara

New City Press

To my parents
Joe and Sharron Markey.
Their loving communion with one another
and with God created the hope and possibility
of great unity and true faith in me and my brothers and sisters.

Published in the United States by New City Press
202 Cardinal Rd., Hyde Park, NY 12538
www.newcitypress.com
©2003 John Markey

Cover design by Nick Cianfarani

Library of Congress Cataloging-in-Publication Data:
  Markey, John J.
  Creating communion : the theology of the constitutions of the church / John J. Markey.
      p. cm.
    ISBN 1-56548-179-8
    1. Church--History of doctrines--20th century. 2. Vatican Council (2nd: 1962-1965) 3.
  Catholic Church--Doctrines--History--20th century. I. Title

BX1746 .M356 2003
262'.02--dc21   2002033712

Printed in Canada

Contents

Foreword (*Thomas F. O'Meara, O.P.*) 9

Introduction 15
   The Problem 18
   The Intuitive Grasp of "Communion" as a Unifying
      Theme 21
   Discerning the Genuine Meaning of Communion 22
   The Structure of This Book 25
   Notes 26

**Chapter 1: Roman Catholic Theology of the Church
      Prior to Vatican II** 27
   I. Ecclesiologies Before Vatican II 30
      A. The Viewpoint of the Counter-Reformation 30
      B. The Church as a "Perfect Society" (*Societas Perfecta*) 32
      C. The Spirit-Animated Organism of Möhler and the
         Tubingen School 35
   II. *Mystici Corporis Christi:* Pope Pius XII's Encyclical on
      the Body of Christ 37
      A. Central Concerns 38
      B. Mystical Body as the Primary Metaphor 39
      C. New Questions 40
      D. The Impact on Theology 43
   III. The Ecclesiology of Yves Congar, O.P. 44
   IV. Toward a Deeper Ecclesiology on the Eve of Vatican II:
      The Church is a Communion by Jerome Hamer, O.P. . 48
   Notes 50

Chapter 2: The Ecclesiology of the Constitutions on the Church 53

I. An Ecclesiology Out of the Documents 53

II. *Sacrosanctum Concilium* 54

III. *Lumen Gentium* 56
    Chapter 1: The Mystery of the Church 58
    Chapter 2: The People of God 60
    Chapter 3: The Church is Hierarchical 66
    Chapter 4: The Laity 74
    Chapter 5: The Call to Holiness 75
    Chapter 6: Religious 77
    Chapter 7: The Pilgrim Church 78
    Chapter 8: Our Lady 78

IV. Summaries of Some Decrees and Declarations
    Bridging *Lumen Gentium* and *Gaudium et Spes* 80
    Unitatis Redintegratio, Christus Dominus, Nostra Aetate,
        and *Apostolicam Actuositatem* 80
    Dignitatis Humanae 82

V. *Gaudium et Spes* 84
    Title and Preface 85
    Introduction: The Situation of Man in the World
        Today 86
    Part I: The Church and Man's Vocation 87
    Part II: Some More Urgent Problems 92
    Conclusion 93

VI. Three Heuristic Keys to the Documents: Three
    Interrelated Concepts 94
    A. Theological Foundation: Renewed Pneumatology . 95
    B. Dominant Image: Community 95
    C. Organizing Concept: Sacramentality 97

Notes 98

Chapter 3: Understanding the Triad that Creates Communion. 100

Introduction. 100

Part I: The Holy Spirit—The Giver of Life 103
The Holy Spirit in Scripture 103
Pneumatology in the Theological Tradition 115
Pneumatology and Spirituality 117
Pneumatology and the Charisms 119
Conclusion: The Work of the Spirit in the Church
and the World 121
Communion Pneumatology 124

Part II: Community—"Members One of Another" . . . 126
Understanding the Conditions for Genuine
Community: The Philosophy of Josiah Royce . 127
The Three Essential Charisms that Create and
Sustain Community 138
Constituting the Christian Community 140
Defining the Church of Christ as a Community of
Communities 142

Part III: Sacrament and Sacramentality—The Church
as a Sign of the Reign of God 147
Symbolic Structure of All Reality. 148
Types of Signs 150
The Chain of Sacramentality and the Catholic
World View. 153
Sacrament and the Seven Sacraments 155
The Special Sacramentality of the Word in the
Catholic Tradition 158
The Church as a Genuine *Icon* of Christ 159
The Significance of the Church in the Post-Modern
World. 161

Conclusion: Communion and the Pneumatological
Principle 165

Notes. 168

**Chapter 4: The Church as the Sacrament of
Communion for the World** 170

Lumen Gentium and *Gaudium et Spes:* The Constitutions
of the Church in the World 171

The Church as a "Sure Seed of Unity, Hope, and
Salvation for the Whole Human Race" 171

The Role of the Church in the Post-Modern and
Hyper-Modern World 173

Notes 184

Acknowledgments 185

Foreword

John Markey presents the Church in history and culture. He has an extensive knowledge of and a true sympathy with the flow of philosophical and theological ideas. This permits him to present well the past as contemporary and accessible to the present reality. His narrative of the theologians and texts of the Council are particularly successful, because they present idea and context, age and seminal implication. In a vivid way he shows what is central and perduring in those theologies of the twentieth century surrounding Vatican II, and in its documents.

The concept of "creation" embedded in the title affirms that this book is a contemporary ecclesiology. Chapter 2 is about theologians who are still prominent and magisterial because they have not been surpassed; the conciliar texts here are not Latin canons but an explosion, an event; above all, they are seeds. The chapters do not summarize or expound but revitalize and express the recent past.

The pages are "post-conciliar" in new ways. They are not only historical cultural but American and experiential. This ecclesiology, as the opening pages point out (as had Markey's words in *America* in 1994, an article still much read), expresses the theology of someone living, educated, and active in teaching and ministry after the Council.

This is a theology of experience: a theology of the author's experience of the Church's experience. Here "experience" means not the feared sense of emotion or the exaggerated charism from the recent past; those fears were nourished by a sad and shallow mechanics of neo-scholasticism before 1960 and are now often reappearing in the overly negative critiques of some scholars. It is experience in the sense of language and thought-forms, culture and age. Each person lives in a world of referential systems and thinks out of mental structures from

science or art, uses a language with creative but limited interpretive possibilities. Looking at the world and understanding
its mode of life gives an experience born of thought-form and
correlation.

Interestingly the conciliar theologians joined what theologians might view as quite distinct: the theology of the Church
and the theology of grace. They saw that the acceptance of the
history of Church forms and the history of human life requires
and implies a return to a deeper theology of grace. Historical
forms means that grace contacts people indeed through the
forms of liturgy and Church but always in ways that are nourished by and subject to the underlying, real but divinely
present horizon or atmosphere of grace, what Jesus called the
kingdom of God. There has been a marked movement away
from grace calculated in an extrinsicist mechanics to the
deeper activity of God in liturgy, ministry, and spirituality.
Congar observes that such a presence of the Spirit produces
both Christian humanism and social action. "This church [of
this or that age, of Europe] is not the only church for the
journey of the human race. The way is basically open [for
other churches to flourish] because and since the Son of God
became man and sent us the Spirit from God. . . ."[1] One of Karl
Rahner's great contributions was to lead the world's Catholics
back to the idea that just as we experience life and existence as
our encompassing world, we experience revelation and grace
not first in things and laws but in deep encounters with the
Holy Spirit present in our personality. Jesus' preaching of the
reign of God occurs first at the level of the experience of his
hearers' religion and life, and offers what "salvation" means
beneath the activities and propositions of a particular religion.
The movement of God expressed in Jesus' stories, later is articulated in words and objects. (Every fundamentalism identities
its privileged clothes and objects and rites at the expense of the
deeper divine reality meeting in experience the human personality.) Ecclesiology serves grace, and grace ultimately is not the
Newtonian and scholastic mechanics of a deity but the

presence of the Spirit as person. The Sabbath of religious things exists not for itself but to serve the human person.

Vatican II proved to be endlessly seminal, and its unfolding implications argued for a dynamic presence of the Spirit. In 1970, Congar wrote that "the work of the Council is a half-way station," and that "the post-conciliar period has so little to do with the Council. . . . The post-conciliar questions are new and radical, and [now] *aggiornamento* means changes and adaptations to a new situation, assuming the principles of the original institution."[2] Markey treats seminal principles as he explores, explains, and illumines areas set in motion by Vatican II. Karl Lehmann, Cardinal Bishop of Mainz, with his usual perceptivity finds in the Council a threefold perduring process: reflection on the signs of the times, the evaluation of healthy enterprises, and a profound renewal of religious and spiritual foundation.[3] Thereby local churches can fashion their own structures of mission.

Postconciliar thinking and life are not mainly propositional; nor are they a hermeneutics of the text. There have been no canonical applications, no tidy new church with vestments, etc. In the United States the great areas of post-conciliar metamorphosis appeared in Church authority, Church ministry, liturgy, social ethics, biological ethics. Europeans visiting America searched in vain for large tomes on God or method but found plans for pastoral areas derived from the American context. Markey's book is American: it remains with those typical American areas, and it draws on American thinkers for ways of imagining communion and faith. He uses the work of Donald Gelpi, S.J., to develop a systematic pneumatology; the thought of Josiah Royce to think clearly and consistently about community, and that of C. S. Peirce to draw out the theology and reality of sacramentality that received much attention before and after Vatican II.

At the same time, Markey stands in the Dominican tradition. In the thirteenth century Albert and Aquinas pondered how to relate modest directions of proper political independence to hierarchy, that is, how to defend the autonomy of both

Church and state, in line with Aristotelian alternatives to Dionysian Platonism. In the twentieth century there is the historic tradition of Church life pursued so extensively and successfully by the approaches of M. D. Chenu, Congar, and Edward Schillebeeckx.

There remain from the Council, or better, there are drawn from today's world and Church by the impetus of the Council two great issues, two areas for ecclesiology today: the quest for a more participatory model of leadership at various levels of the Church and the continued realization of the local Church with its parishes as the Body of Christ with ordained ministries and lay ecclesial ministries.

Drawing on his American sources, Markey offers communion as a "real" and a "practical" alternative to these fundamental issues. For the first time he shows how government and authority need to be based on open and honest dialogue, mutual trust, shared charisms, genuine accountability at all levels. This results in a sense of participation in some way by all the members of the community. To the second he offers a balanced and practical account of the relationship between the universal and the local church. He stresses the importance of the fullness of the local church in all its dimensions as the condition of the possibility of achieving that kind of universal salvific community which the Spirit—in and out of time—calls the Church of Christ to be.

Vatican II marked the Catholic Church's acceptance of history. The Church lives in time. "The vision of the Council," Yves Congar wrote, "has been resolutely that of the history of salvation completed by eschatology."[4] The modern human person lives in history and does not simply move through chronological time. Since the Council affirmed "the acceptance of the historicity of the Church,"[5] the Christian community does not just exhibit but is itself a process of visible sacramentality in forms, ecclesial as well as liturgical. So there has not been just one liturgy, in Latin after 1600, or one theology of grace, in French after 1750. The Church had always had variety and change, and in recent decades history has been inviting her to escape her prison of forms that were not ancient but recent.

Historical moments such as the present can be unnerving, although change is not always oppressive and frightening. Congar in the last decade of his life frequently observed: "The years after the Council are a global phenomenon with world-wide dimensions. A crisis would have come anyway. The Council assisted its entry into the Church by ending the isolation of the Church, by giving a wider audience to the Church, and by ending a monolithic institution protected by fictions. The present time is linked to the gigantic changes touching culture, the way of life in societies, and the shared humanity of the world."[5] Precisely when the Church ignores her mission in the world and in history, she is most vulnerable to the ravages of time; for nature and human life are shot through with change. If the Church tries to hold back history and neurotically assumes the mask of an age dead or dying, history appears harsh. The Church is not a club or a museum, and history, while showing the wounds and failings of the Church, brings survival and life. A rigid obedience to the past is not fidelity but anxiety. To know history is to be set free. In the Church today, in a parish whether American or Nigerian, there should be a sense of history, of rediscovering an earlier time in the Church, of letting go of the nineteenth century, of the twentieth century.

The Pauline letters state that the interior gift of the Spirit owns some modest creativity toward history and culture, so that the community may continue to incarnate itself invisibly and visibly. If the blood of the Church is history, the flesh of the community of Christ is culture. The history of the Church offers not a set of laws, the same old successful or static realizations, but new forms of cultural history. The size and opportunities of the Church today are vastly different from the ones of even thirty years ago. The culture of an age offers principles of Church life and self-interpretation,[6] forms through which the Church acts on behalf of the kingdom of God. The Word of God assumes the culture of a particular tradition, selecting a language to express reality, a landscape, and a ritual for liturgy. The Church lives within cultures, because human beings are effectively addressed and personally touched within their psychic and cultural worlds. The sacred space and holy symbols of this architecture invites the Spirit.

Ultimately, Markey offers us a fresh insight and systematic clarification of this Spirit-permeated and historically grounded Church that Vatican II envisioned in such a new and dramatic way.

Thomas F. O'Meara, O.P.
Professor Emeritus, University of Notre Dame
Author of *The Theology of Ministry*

Notes

1. "Situation ecclésiologique au moment de 'Ecclesiam suan' et passage à une Église dans l'itinéraire des hommes," *Le Concile de Vatican II* (Paris: Beauchesne, 1984) 32.
2. Private letter from Congar to the author (December 9, 1970).
3. "Situation ecclésiologique . . ." 27.
4. *Fifty Years of Catholic Theology: Conversations with Yves Congar*, B. Laurent, ed. (Philadelphia: Fortress, 1988) 3f.
5. Congar, "Une passion." *L'unité* (Paris: Cerf, 1974) 109.
6. Congar, *Le Concile au jour le jour* [Session IV] (Paris: Cerf, 1966) 61.

Introduction

> . . . the whole world expects a step forward toward a
> doctrinal penetration and a formation of consciences
> in the faithful and perfect conformity to the authentic
> doctrine which, however, should be studied and
> expounded through the methods of research and
> through the literary forms of modern thought. The
> substance of the ancient doctrine of the Deposit of
> Faith is one thing, and the way in which it is presented
> is another. And it is the latter that must be taken into
> great consideration, with patience if necessary, every-
> thing being measured in the forms and proportions of
> a magisterium which is predominantly pastoral in
> character.

Pope John XXIII, October 11, 1962

These words, in the context of an opening address which
inaugurated one of the most profound religious and social
events of the twentieth century, have, in retrospect, shaped and
informed my religious experience, and I believe those of my
generation, as much as anything written or said at that historic
Council. I have had the privilege, though some would claim the
misfortune, of coming to my intellectual and religious maturity
in a Church struggling to realize the great task set before her in
that address. For all of my conscious life my community of faith
has been trying to study, expound, and present that immense
and varied Deposit of Faith in terms of the "modern" mind and
the pastoral needs of a truly worldwide communion of faith.

I was born two weeks before the pope issued the document
officially convoking the Council, and I entered kindergarten at
All Souls Catholic School in Englewood, Colorado, less than a
year after the Council officially ended. I would go on to attend

Catholic primary and secondary school, a Catholic college, teach in a Catholic high school and parish, join a religious order, go to seminary, be ordained to the priesthood, write a dissertation on Catholic ecclesiology for my doctorate in systematic theology, and reach the point where I am currently teaching theology at a Catholic university.

I have never attended a Latin Mass and was never taught the *Baltimore Catechism*; I was not imbued from an early age with "Catholic guilt" and have never gone to confession in the "box" (as a matter of fact the first time that I was even in the traditional confessional was to *hear* confessions after I was ordained); I have no memory of "meatless Fridays" except occasionally during Lent; and although I have attended Catholic school my whole life and have been taught by many religious sisters and brothers (none of whom wore a full habit other than an occasional veil), I have never experienced them to be mean, angry or abusive; on the contrary, I have always found them to be among the most interesting, compassionate, and entertaining teachers and mentors, and am sure that it was the combination of dedication, camaraderie, and joy I witnessed in my early and secondary education that led me, eventually, to my present state in life.

It has occurred to me that I am among the first of a generation raised and educated entirely in a post-Vatican II context; a context which seems to be, to say the least, profoundly different from that of the era which immediately preceded it. My life, education, and journey of faith have paralleled that of the Church since Vatican II. As I approach my fortieth birthday, I have found myself increasingly looking back on my life and evaluating the choices and decisions that have led me to this place in my life. I am also looking forward in an effort to discern the general trajectory of my life and find within it a sense of purpose and direction; not because I believe that I am coming to the end of something but, rather, that some new and important stage of my life is beginning. The Church also seems to have reached a point in her life where a similar process is taking place.

By any estimation the Second Vatican Council was overwhelmingly successful. The world-wide membership of the Church has increased dramatically since the Council and now approaches one billion people. The Church has opened relationships and friendly dialogues with almost every Christian denomination and world religion, yielding genuinely fruitful results in many surprising and hopeful ways. There are more people ministering in the Church and on behalf of the Church today than at any previous time in history. The dramatic and unprecedented growth in lay participation at all levels in the life of the Church surely serves as a primary indication of the guidance of the Holy Spirit on the Council and its aftermath. The Church both local and universal now finds herself deeply involved in the lives of people in ways that would have been unthinkable or much more limited before the Council (i.e., social service, political advocacy, health services, education, care for refugees, mediation for peace, defense of human rights and social justice, spiritual guidance and direction, etc.). Moreover, its service extends not only to Catholics but also to other Christians, believers of various faiths, and to all dimensions of the human family.

Vatican II marked a great new moment in the life of the Church. It serves as the foundation or "blueprint" for the Church's development in the coming centuries, and it is clearly not over yet. To study this Council, its documents, and underlying theology is not just a study of history, but is in fact a critical reflection upon the most immediate reality of Christian life. All of the members of the Church (and even those who appear to be outside of it) have an important stake in this unfolding event. The process of renewal and transformation begun in the early 1960's will continue for many years and even centuries to come.

This book is my own attempt to look both back and forward: back on the origins, primary theological content, and practical implications of Vatican II; forward to the next stage in the life of the Church, offering some theological reflections to help other Catholics to participate in this process.

The Problem

As with any immensely successful event, there are also problems, difficulties, and misunderstandings that have arisen.
Dramatic growth and change inevitably raise questions about
balancing these elements with the need for stability and secu-
rity. One cannot expect a billion people to be transformed
overnight.

One day, right after I was ordained, I was standing outside in
the church parking lot talking with a woman I would describe
reverently as "middle aged." She was distressed about some
aspect of parish life or another (as occasionally we all are), and
she said suddenly, without anger or spite, but wistfully and even
poignantly, "Some days I really miss the Church I grew up in." I
understood and appreciated her feelings at that moment quite
clearly, for these days I, too, miss the Church of my childhood.
Growing up in the 70's the Church was for me an invigorating
and exciting place. Our parish and school were growing and
developing; they offered rich and new ideas and opportunities to
both me and my parents. We embraced that Church, a Church
where anything seemed possible. It was during that time that my
love for theology and hope for greater participation in the life of
the Church was born and kindled. I believed that it was spring-
time in the life of the Church, and I looked forward to a future of
planting, growing and reaping in her fields.

In the years since college I have watched a growing polariza-
tion of the Church and increasing antagonism between the
ideological left and the right. While many of the things that I
took for granted about the Church of my childhood have
remained the same, other realities have been called into question or changed. I have personally discovered that no single
interpretation or experience (and certainly not my own) can
exhaust the richness of what the Council bequeathed to us.
The Church as a whole entered into a more somber and intro-
spective period, a season marked not as much by growth and
expansion but by pruning and refining. This realization has

led me to conclude that what I experienced as a child and adolescent was not the spring, but the Indian summer of a long autumn. I feel, at times, that we have entered the winter season in the life of the Church; a season of which I have never been particularly fond.

I am not comfortable in winter, but I am quite hopeful for the Church. Some people, including John Paul II, even see a spring-time arising in the Church. In either case, important and necessary things happen in the winter, and we are not the first generation of Christians in general and Catholics in particular who have weathered this season, or reaped its fruits. I also realize that the current situation in the Church is the inevitable result of a fundamental reorientation in the life of such a large, diverse and complex community of faith. Like the life of the human body, the corporate Body of Christ went through a kind of new birth forty years ago. It has emerged over the years through the awkward stages of childhood and adolescence, the rebellion and discovery of the teenage and early adult years, the burden of new responsibilities that come with maturity and struggling with difficult decisions, the mistakes and sobering realities that full adulthood brings. Like myself, the Church can assess her years of growth and prepare for the future that awaits her.

At the dawn of the new millennium, the Church finds herself faced with a number of problems and crises rooted in previous centuries—problems both religious and universal in scope. In many ways, the work of the Second Vatican Council, coming at the end of the last millennium, serves as a gift to encourage and guide the Church in this new era. The proximity of Vatican II to the new millennium symbolically represents its place in the history of the Church; it marks both the end of one long era of development and the beginning of another. Most significantly, at Vatican II the whole Church took time to stop and seriously reflect on the two thousand years that had elapsed since the life, death, and resurrection of Jesus Christ and the giving over of his Spirit to create the Church. The Church sought to recognize her growth and development as a living reality developing through history under the guidance of the Holy Spirit, and also as a sinful prodigal always in need of repentance and renewal. By critically examining its past and seriously facing the future, the Church at Vatican II was able for the first time in her history to synthesize and formulate her self-understanding in a fundamental and systematic way.

This process led to the writing and ratification of four Constitutions (as well as numerous Declarations and Decrees). These Constitutions (particularly the two on the nature and mission of the Church itself: *Lumen Gentium* and *Gaudium et Spes*) represent a genuinely new level of self-consciousness and theological articulation in the life of the Church. This is not to say that the Church had not previously understood her nature and mission correctly, nor that she had not had a tradition of formal articulation of this self-understanding. Nevertheless, previous to Vatican II the Church had only spoken about her own life in limited and partial ways, usually in response to some specific crisis or question. At Vatican II there was an attempt to describe the full scope of the nature and mission of the Church in both her internal and external dimensions. The Constitutions, therefore, stand as the result of two thousand years of theological reflection and as the beginning of many new centuries of theological investigation and pastoral service. These Constitutions helped to free the Church from much of the acrimonious, narrow, and defensive posturing that had troubled her since the time of the Reformation and Counter-Reformation, as well as the fear and doubt that pervaded her confrontation with modernity. They have also irreversibly opened the Church to an exciting but uncertain future.

There remains an ongoing need to ensure that the valid traditions grounding the Constitutions are not supplanted by false or limited innovations that disrupt or divide the common life of the faithful. At the heart of most of the controversies within the Church that have followed the Council have been questions concerning unity and diversity. This question—as old as the history of philosophy and theology themselves—lies at the very heart of the Constitutions but cannot be simply resolved by appealing to one text or another. It is only with a deep appreciation for the full content of the Council documents and their organizing vision that a common understanding of the balance between continuity and change, growth and stability, unity and diversity may emerge.

Ideologies referred to as the Left and the Right, or Liberal and Conservative, have been struggling since the Council to interpret its operational consequences in a way consistent with their particular frame of reference. While the struggles between various constituencies within the wider Church initially represent a possible crisis of unity, a charitable and ongoing discussion, engaging numerous points of view, is the inevitable result of a significant shift in the life of such a large and unique reality. Both sides have actually rendered a service to the Church in that they have pointed out the complexities and ambiguities of the documents themselves, and the many dynamic possibilities and issues that must be worked out through the living experience of the whole Church. The differing opinions have also shown the high level of consensus and convergence that already exists within the Church on the basic doctrines and beliefs that ground the documents. Furthermore, they have pointed out what is genuinely new and inspired in the Constitutions and needs deeper exploration and investigation. Nowhere is this unique point of common theological investigation clearer than in the concept of "communion," which commentators from all sides of the theological spectrum and from many ecumenical perspectives have claimed as central to the proper interpretation of Vatican II.

The Intuitive Grasp of "Communion" as a Unifying Theme

"The concept of communion (*koinonia*), which appears with a certain prominence in the texts of the Second Vatican Council, is very suitable for expressing the core mystery of the Church and can certainly be a key for the renewal of Catholic ecclesiology."[1] This statement, which comes from a 1992

Congregation for the Doctrine of the Faith (CDF) document on communion, echoes and elaborates on an earlier and more direct statement contained in the Final Report of the Extraordinary Synod of Bishops meeting in 1985, called to "reflect" on Vatican II: "The ecclesiology of *communion* is the central and fundamental idea of the council's documents."[2] Both the CDF document and the text of the Synod emphasize that the richness of this concept lies in its ability to integrate the sacramental, and therefore supernatural, dimension of the Church with that aspect of the Church which is "an organically structured community" analogous to other types of natural social unions.[3] This dual nature makes the Church a particularly unique and complex reality that demands a sophisticated and nuanced interpretation by those within and outside her. The aforementioned statements demonstrate the growing importance of what in Roman Catholic thought has become known as "communion ecclesiology." The ascendancy of this theology of the Church (ecclesiology) is due to a variety of factors, the most compelling of which is its ability to directly address the new issues emerging in the Roman Catholic Church after Vatican II. The concept of communion bears directly on ecclesial questions both internal and ecumenical in scope. Communion ecclesiology, therefore, presents a rich and fruitful "point of entry" to the most pertinent challenges facing the Church and the reflection on her identity.

Discerning the Genuine Meaning of Communion

A number of commentators have perceived that while agreeing on the term "communion" in principle, there are a variety of interpretations of the actual meaning and concrete consequences of this understanding of the Church. The various points of view described above often disagree about the direction for the future that such an ecclesiology mandates. This growing and intensifying debate is rooted in the documents of Vatican II themselves. While both the texts and the "spirit" of the Council indeed suggest what has come to be known as communion ecclesiology, nowhere did the Council actually name and systematically develop this ecclesiology. Furthermore, even the vocabulary, now so widespread in most theological discussions of the Church, cannot be described as consistently employed nor systematically defined. The central relationship between the terms "communion" (*communio* in Latin) and "community" (*communitas* in Latin) evoke a number of interpretations; and the terms themselves, while verbally distinct, are often used interchangeably in the documents and in the work of subsequent commentators. These fundamentally analogous terms are shaped by their context and in conjunction with other metaphors and adjectives. This means that while the concept of communion is a rich source of theological reflection, it is also a term that in itself lacks any genuine clarity.

Consequently, much of the Roman Catholic ecclesiology emerging out of Vatican II, which has enthusiastically embraced this new emphasis on communion and community, has often uncritically inherited an underlying lack of clarity. The next stage in theological reflection must take care not to simply adopt the terminology of communion without fully examining its meaning or the relationships between it and other related concepts. The goal of this book, therefore, is to trace out the development of this concept from its roots in the tradition, through its underlying presence in the documents of the Council, to some of the practical and concrete implications for the future of the Church.

I contend that communion ecclesiology amounts to what others have called a Copernican revolution in ecclesiology in that it challenges and reinterprets almost every dimension of the Church's self-understanding. This fact demands not only a thorough and systematic recovery of the New Testament and the traditional theological sources of this theology, but a new interpretation of the foundational principles that ground this ecclesiology and its broader context. Community and communion emerge as leading ideas and guiding principles of the

Council's definition of the Church, and the parameters of this ecclesiology are indeed embedded in the Vatican II documents themselves, but not in a simplistic or overt way. The starting point for a sound communion ecclesiology must begin with a more subtle reading of the significant texts of the Council, putting them in their proper historical and broader theological context.

I believe, however, that a proper interpretation of the conciliar documents invokes some basic theological concepts. A greater understanding of the idea of communion itself may help resolve some of the differences in regard to the critical implications of communion ecclesiology and expand this ecclesiology to meet the challenges arising out of both internal and ecumenical ecclesial discussions. Developing a foundational understanding of communion and examining its ecclesial implications can refocus the current dialogue in a more critical and fruitful direction.

Communion is a complex and far-reaching term, because it denotes the triadic (three-way) relationship between the theology of the Holy Spirit (called pneumatology), community and sacrament. I contend that these three concepts were the leading or guiding ideas of the Council that can be seen working together throughout the documents to enrich and fulfill many areas of traditional Catholic doctrine. Communion almost always refers to a *community* that is filled with and empowered by the *Spirit* of God and lives through the sharing of gifts and charisms inspired by the Spirit in such a way that it acts as both a *sign and instrument* of God's saving plan for the universal community. In other words, communion means the relationship between the Spirit, a local community and that local community's relationship to all other local communities, and their sacramental relationship to the world. The Church exists as a communion precisely when and because she embodies this complex relationship.

The Structure of This Book

The first chapter of this work lays out the dominant ecclesiology prevalent in the Roman Catholic Church in the one hundred years preceding the Second Vatican Council, paying particular attention to the sources and development of the ecclesiology of the "Mystical Body of Christ," particularly as it is articulated in the papal encyclical *Mystici Corporis Christi*.[4] I shall also explore its development in the seminal work of the theologians Yves Congar, O.P., and Jerome Hamer, O.P.[5]

The second chapter examines, in some detail, the documents of the Second Vatican Council, particularly the two texts devoted explicitly to the Constitution of the Church (*Lumen Gentium* and *Gaudium et Spes,*[6]) drawing out those lines of thought consistent with or corrective of earlier interpretations of the Church. I also suggest an overall schema influenced by the ecclesiology of Congar and Hamer, which offers an interpretive key to the underlying unity between the two constitutions and the other documents. This schema presents a definition of communion as the interrelationship between Spirit, community, and sacrament and, therefore, contends that communion, understood in this way, indeed acts as the unifying thread running throughout the documents.

The third chapter delves into the history and meaning of the component parts of the triad that creates genuine communion. A more thorough examination of the theology of the Holy Spirit, a dynamic definition of community, and the importance of sacraments and sacramentality, elaborates on the unique nature of communion and clarifies some of the many issues surrounding the term by offering guidelines for a proper understanding of this concept. This investigation also suggests some guidelines for faithfully interpreting the Council.

The fourth and final chapter assesses some of the challenges that face the Church at the beginning of a new era. One of the most significant changes that has taken place since the Council has been what many social commentators have called a shift from a modern to a post-modern culture in many parts of the world. This fundamental shift in culture implies an even greater urgency to the mission of the Church articulated at Vatican II. There is, it seems, a deep connection between the realization of the Church as a communion and the prospects for the New Evangelization called for by Pope John Paul II.[7] The conviction of the council fathers that the futures of the Church and the world are inextricably linked, ultimately means that communion offers a means of unity, peace and hope to all of humanity.

Notes

1. Congregation for the Doctrine of the Faith (henceforth CDF). "Some Aspects of the Church Understood as Communion." *Origins* 22 (June 25, 1992): Introduction, 1, 108.
2. National Conference of Catholic Bishops, *The Final Report of the Extraordinary Synod of Bishops, Rome, 1985* (Washington D.C.: United States Catholic Conference, Inc., 1986), C, 1.
3. CDF, "Some Aspects of the Church," I, 3.
4. Pope Pius XII, *Mystici Corporis Christi*, in *Acta Apostolica Sedis*, 35 (1943), 193–248. English translation: *The Papal Encyclicals 1939–1958*, ed. Claudia Carlen (Wilmington, N.C.: McGrath, 1981) 35–63. Hereafter referred to as MCC.
5. I have chosen these two theologians, who happen to both be Dominicans, because they make the categories of communion and community central to their pre-Vatican II ecclesiologies. Avery Dulles, S.J., similarly chooses Congar and Hamer as representative of his second model of the Church, "The Church as Mystical Communion," in his book *Models of the Church* (Garden City, New York: Doubleday and Company, 1974) 43–57; revised edition (New York: Image Books, 1987) 47–62. While almost all other major theologians writing between *Mystici Corporis* and Vatican II incorporate the themes of communion and community in their work (de Lubac, Rahner, Danielou, Bouyer, etc.) they do not make it as fundamentally central as the two theologians I have chosen.
6. *Vatican Council II: The Conciliar and Post-Conciliar Documents*, Austin Flannery, O.P., ed., The New Revised Study Edition (New York: Costello Publishing Co., 1992). *Lumen Gentium: Dogmatic Constitution on the Church* (1964) 350–432, hereafter referred to as LG; *Gaudium et Spes: Pastoral Constitution on the Church in the Modern World* (1965) 903–1000, hereafter referred to as GS.
7. John Paul II, *At the Beginning of the New Millennium, Novo Millenio Ineunte*, issued January 6, 2001. *Origins* 30 (January 18, 2001), 31.

Chapter 1

Roman Catholic Theology of the Church Prior to Vatican II

Augustine was made bishop of the diocese of Hippo in Northern Africa in 395 A.D. and remained there until his death in 430 A.D. Born in 354, he spent most of his life trying to reconcile the demands of the gospel with the fact that the Church had literally been merged with the Roman Empire, one of the largest and most powerful empires in human history. Furthermore, even as he struggled with the process of bringing together two such different world views, the Empire itself was under siege from external forces and collapsing from internal decay. It was during this complex period, toward the end of his life and with "barbarians" literally at the gates of the city of Hippo, that Augustine, one of the last and perhaps greatest theologians of the patristic era, wrote one of his final and most significant works: *The City of God*.[1]

The City of God represents Augustine's mature reflection upon the profound effects of original sin on human history and God's plan of salvation in the light of this devastation. He sees the world as divided into two cities. First, the city of Cain or human city is composed of those who have chosen to turn away from God and to follow their own passions and self-indulgence. This city is only concerned with temporal and material affairs and is usually quite successful at it. Second, the city of God is composed of those who, through no merit of their own, have been chosen by God to follow his plan of salvation revealed in Christ and, therefore, to live the life of the blessed ones here on earth. This second city is a minority living within the city of Cain, and humans are often unaware of who is a member of which city. The city of God has a special connection to the visible Church, although mere membership in the Church does not in itself guarantee citizenship. Against any moral complacency, Augustine insists that only a life of genuine self-sacrifice and self-renunciation serves as a sign of divine citizenship. In his view there are two worlds living side by side in one human history. History itself is a process, not of saving or converting one to the other, but of sorting out the two, at the end of time each going off to their proper end. The great mass of humanity belonging to the city of Cain/ humanity will be sent to endure everlasting torment; the holy remnant of the city of God will be granted the vision of God and eternal joy. Much like Noah's ark,[2] the Church's sole function in the world is to bring the saved to their reward and to keep the traditions and beliefs of the blessed ones secure in a world ravaged by sin and chaos. In such a dualistic vision of reality, the Church has no choice but to focus on "spiritual" realities and to strive to preserve its unique, divinely revealed patrimony.

In many ways, this work became one of Augustine's most important legacies to the Church. For almost fifteen hundred years it functioned unofficially, and often unconsciously, as a kind of underlying constitution shaping the primary way for viewing the Church's relationship to the world. In the dualistic understanding of the Church's relationship created by *The City of God*, the Church, whether visible or invisible, was separate and distinct from the rest of the world. This meant that Church and world, the spiritual and the temporal, the sacred and the profane, the holy and the ordinary, comprised two fundamentally different, even if related, aspects of history and, hence, of human experience. A series of great Councils and historical disputes between the eleventh century and the Council of Trent (late seventeenth century) would mostly shape the internal structures and offices of the Church and the way in which local churches and the universal Church would relate to one another, leaving virtually unchallenged the fundamentally dualistic presumption about the relationship between the Church and the world.

This dualistic world-view set the Church in a conflictual relationship with the secular and political realms. Ironically, questions about Church/state relations, the organization of secular society and the Church within it, and the rights of either dimension vis-à-vis the other, dominated western ecclesiology throughout much of the Middle Ages. It was only through the fracturing of the unity of the Western Church during the Reformation and the diminishment of the Church's power and influence with the coming of modernity that the Roman Catholic Church had to face a whole new set of ecclesiological questions and problems. This change in orientation and perspective caused the Church to undertake a dramatic self-examination and to discover a deeper level of self-understanding.

In this chapter, I will briefly sketch the model of ecclesiology that dominated the Roman Catholic Church's self-understanding from the time of the Counter-Reformation until the mid-twentieth century, particularly as formulated in the mid-nineteenth century. Secondly, I will outline the recovery and development of a substratum labeled "Mystical Body of Christ ecclesiology," which began in the early nineteenth century and culminated in 1943 with the publication of the papal encyclical *Mystici Corporis Christi*.[3] The third part will summarize and analyze this encyclical, pointing out the new orientation it sanctioned in Roman Catholic thought. Finally, I will describe the ecclesiology espoused by Yves Congar, O.P., and Jerome Hamer, O.P., in the years immediately preceding the Council, an ecclesiology which systematically developed and popularized the concepts of community and communion.

I. Ecclesiologies Before Vatican II

A. The Viewpoint of the Counter-Reformation

The ecclesiology dominant in Roman Catholic official and conciliar statements, and in the theological manuals and texts between the Council of Trent and Vatican II, is often portrayed as a simple and monolithic apologetic. It is described as maintaining the necessity of the visible structures of the Church for salvation, the primacy and power of the papacy for apostolic validity and, hence, the unquestionable presumption that only the Roman Catholic Church is to be identified with the Church created by Jesus Christ, and organized and institutionalized under the guidance of his personally chosen apostles and their successors. While for almost three hundred years after the Council of Trent most Roman Catholic ecclesiology can indeed be described as primarily apologetic and defensive in nature, the description of this ecclesiology as static or monolithic is not entirely accurate. The ecclesiology evident in the documents and texts from the time of the Counter-Reformation until Vatican Council I was largely the result of the Church responding, with increasing stridency, to a long series of crises and controversies that shaped both the tenor and the doctrinal emphasis of ecclesiology. As the outstanding historical surveys of both Yves Congar[4] and Louis Bouyer[5] illustrate, the ecclesiology that characterized the mid-nineteenth century developed gradually. First it did so in response to Protestantism, then in response to the nationalist ideologies of Jansenism/ Gallicanism, Febronianism, and Josephism,[6] and finally in reaction to the radical European cultural transition caused by the French Revolution.

These historical and cultural forces eventually led Catholic ecclesiology to fall under two principal rubrics. On the one hand, Protestants stressed the invisible and inward character of the Church and were therefore seen as ultimately rejecting the whole of the Church's mediatory powers (i.e., magisterium, priesthood, sacraments, episcopal power and papal primacy). Against this view, Roman Catholic theologians emphasized the fundamentally visible, sacramental, and hierarchical nature of the Church (its external structures and their efficacy) almost to the exclusion of any reflection on the less institutional elements of ecclesiology.[7] On the other hand, not only Protestantism but also the nationalist ideologies emerging in the seventeenth and eighteenth centuries called into question both the primacy and legitimacy of any exercise of papal power. In response to this, Roman Catholic theologians defended the absolute necessity and hegemony of the Petrine office as constitutive of the very essence of the Church. Theological and rhetorical foundations for the ecclesiology that integrated these two foci were laid out principally by the Jesuit theologian Robert Bellarmine in the seventeenth century, and were embellished in the manuals and catechisms of the next three centuries.[8]

Congar observes that by the early nineteenth century both Protestant and Catholic theology had evolved into very skewed and diminished versions of the tradition:

> Thus whilst Protestants were reducing the Church to an inward Christianity, to salvation, and by doing so were dissolving ecclesiology, Catholic apologists were looking at her above all as the machinery of the means of grace, as the hierarchical mediation of the means of salvation. . . . The "de Ecclesia" was principally, sometimes almost exclusively, a defense and affirmation of the reality of the Church as machinery of hierarchical mediation, of the powers and the primacy of the Roman see, in a word, a "hierarchology." On the other hand, the two terms between which mediation comes, the Holy Spirit on one side, the faithful people or religious subject on the other, were kept out of ecclesiological consideration.[9]

It was into this milieu that two rather different but innovative ecclesiological syntheses emerged in the nineteenth century: the ecclesiology of the *societas perfecta* and the "Mystical Body" ecclesiology of Johann Möhler.

B. The Church as a "Perfect Society" (*Societas Perfecta*)

The term *societas perfecta* itself can be found fairly early in the theological tradition particularly as a way of describing a desired integration and balance between civil power and ecclesiastical authority in a single, unified social system. In the late eighteenth and early nineteenth century, however, this terminology is re-introduced to describe the self-sufficiency and autonomy of the Roman Catholic Church over against the secular society in which it happens to be located. Historian and ecclesiologist Patrick Granfield, in a series of studies on the concept of *societas perfecta*, concludes that this term evolved over about fifteen centuries until its meaning was almost totally inverted in the late-nineteenth century.[10] Granfield points out that originally the term emerged as a way of describing Church-state relationships from the late Patristic period through the Medieval and the early Counter-Reformation periods of Church history.[11] In this period, the Church and the state were not seen as separate or independent societies, "but rather as two parts of a unified social reality—the *republica christiana*."[12] A perfect society resulted from the proper functioning of two interdependent social units that together constituted a single order. And while there is an ongoing controversy in the history of the Church as to the exact and requisite balance between the power and role of these two social units, they remained theoretically united for over a thousand years.

As the Church found itself increasingly pushed to the margins or directly assaulted by civil powers throughout Europe (as well as in new areas of growth and evangelization like North America), it responded by reinterpreting itself as a separate and distinct society existing alongside, but not dependent on or answerable to, the local and national societies in which it existed. Increasingly, apologists and theologians of the Catholic Church began describing a perfect society as one that "is complete and independent in itself and possesses all the means necessary to attain its proposed end."[13] This innovative view of the Church as a perfect society in itself reached its apex in the first and second drafts of the major schemata on the Church prepared for Vatican I, *Supremis Pastoris* and *Tametsi Deus*.[14] Chapter 3 of *Supremis Pastoris* describes the Church as "a true, perfect, spiritual and supernatural society" that cannot be considered as

> a member or a part of any other society whatsoever nor can it be confused with or mixed with any other society. But it is so perfect in itself that, although it is distinct from all other human societies, it also far surpasses all of them.[15]

After the bishops offered a considerable amount of critique on this draft, the later draft not only reaffirmed the strong language of the first schema but refined it even more clearly:

> [The Church] is a society, distinct from every other assembly of men, which moves towards its proper end by its own way and reasons; which is absolute, complete and sufficient in itself to attain those things which pertain to it; and which is neither subject to, or joined as part, or mixed and confused with any other society.[16]

While neither document was ever officially promulgated by Vatican I (because the Council was interrupted and not resumed), one can safely assert that these statements influenced the tenor and direction of all subsequent Roman Catholic ecclesiology until Vatican II.[17]

The development and popularity of this self-understanding were possible for two reasons. First, with the growth and

diversity of religious orders in the era immediately preceding
the French Revolution and their rapid and unprecedented
expansion in the mid-nineteenth century, the Church was
actually able to operate as a separate society. It had its own
schools, hospitals, social services, fraternal organizations,
governmental systems, etc., and simply did not need the civil
society to meet the basic needs of its members. Secondly, with
the introduction of a new form of Neo-Scholastic theology in
the mid-nineteenth century as a response to Kant and
"modern" philosophy, the Church found the philosophical
and ideological underpinnings needed to ground a new, and
radically dualistic, formulation of the traditional Church/
world relationship.[18] In this sense the Church understood
itself as existing "over-against" the world, in a way analogous
to the relationship of the natural to the supernatural.

Embraced by the magisterium and popes from Pius IX
through Pius XII, this new understanding of the Church as a
perfect society came to be the dominant formulation of
ecclesiology until Vatican II.[19] It was an important development in ecclesiology, because it helped the Church
re-interpret her mission and purpose in light of the radical
changes brought about by modernity. In many ways it was a
rather successful response to the marginalization and denigra-
tion of the Church's role in the civil and public arena of ordinary believers' daily lives. Its disadvantage was that it fostered
a highly juridical and utilitarian ecclesiology that emphasized
the institutional and clerical/hierarchical dimensions of the
Church almost to the exclusion of any other elements.
Furthermore, the dualistic foundations of this ecclesiology
eroded traditional theology by creating a mechanistic view of
grace whereby grace was "distributed" almost exclusively by
the ecclesial institution and its formal structures and rituals.
This likewise fostered a narrowly centralist and gnostic understanding of revelation, which reduced God's personal
self-disclosure in history to those doctrines and their interpretations officially promulgated by the teaching authorities of
the Church. The long-term effect of this ecclesiology was to

isolate the Roman Catholic Church from the other Christian Churches and to place her in an antagonistic relationship with the secular societies for well over a century.

C. The Spirit-Animated Organism of Möhler and the Tubingen School

Johann Adam Möhler (1796–1838) was first a student at the Catholic Seminary at the University of Tubingen, under the tutelage of its most distinguished systematic theologian, Johann Sebastian Drey (1777–1853), and later a professor of theology at the same institution. Drey stood at the beginning of what Thomas O'Meara, O.P., calls "the romantic-idealist renaissance of German Catholicism."[20] Drey, a historian and disciple of the philosopher Schelling and unschooled in older strains of Neo-Scholasticism, worked outside the narrow bounds of most manualist and catechetical theology and introduced into Roman Catholic thought a new set of categories and sources for recovering and analyzing the tradition. Möhler, under the guidance of Drey, was similarly influenced by Schelling (and later by Hegel). Möhler also developed an ecumenical sensibility that allowed him to pursue the work of the theologian Schleiermacher and the historian Neander, which in turn encouraged in him an intense interest in the study of the Patristic sources.[21] In 1825, Möhler brought this wealth of diverse and innovative scholarship to bear on his first great treatise on the Church, *Die Einheit in der Kirche* (Unity in the Church).[22] For Möhler, the starting point of any reflection on the Church should not consist in an elucidation of the juridical and structural aspects of the Church but on the Holy Spirit, who constitutes the fundamental and dynamic "Principle" underlying these structures. The basis of Möhler's ecclesiology is a systematic pneumatology that places the history and concrete tradition of the Church in the context of the unfolding of the life and power of the Spirit in Christian believers. This life is expressed visibly in the diverse persons, books of scripture, doctrines, sacraments, charisms and offices of the Church—like the various organs of a body, though distinct, are animated by a single life principle—but is united in a single, underlying and transcendent Spirit that is shaping all of these diverse activities into a "community of love" that is itself the expression of the divine life.[23]

> The Church, then, is essentially the realization of the divine life, which in its depth is the divine love communicated to mankind by the Holy Spirit. It is from this fact that the evangelical truth is bound up with the Church, that she alone can have truth within herself and communicate it by extending herself to men.[24]

Consequently, far from negating or relativizing the historically developed structures of the Church and the centrality of her "visible" forms, Möhler argues for the validity, even necessity, of these structures as part of the divine plan for salvation.

Möhler, however, describes the Church not as a static institution but as an organism that lives in and through history, and therefore changes, grows and develops over time like all living things. This does not diminish the validity of its truth claims but gives a principle of unity that creates in the Church a dynamic tradition. This tradition unfolds with greater clarity and fruitfulness as the Church defines herself through taking on successive and concrete forms and expressions. There is no fundamental duality, therefore, between genuine growth in knowledge, as expressed in dogma and magisterium, and the inner development of the Christian community as a fellowship of faith, hope and love. This interior spiritual unity of the Church, which is the life and power of the Holy Spirit, is directly manifest in the "organic unity" of the historically acting, visibly interacting community of the Church. For this reason, Möhler finds the Pauline metaphor of the Church as the Mystical Body of Christ most adequate for describing the literal reality of the Church's life—it is an organism comprised of an inner spiritual unity visibly expressed in the external organic unity of her life and acts.[25]

Möhler went on to further develop this idea in his later work entitled, *Symbolism: The Doctrinal Differences between Protestants and Catholics*, which was basically a systematic comparison of Protestant and Catholic thought.[26] After his death his work continued to have great influence in German Catholic circles, particularly at Tubingen. His work also evidently influenced the Roman schools, particularly the work of Carlo Passaglia (1812–1887) and his students, although the exact nature of this relationship is not clear.[27] Through these Roman scholars, this ecclesiology was influential in shaping, for the First Vatican Council, the initial draft of the schema *De Ecclesia*, which would ultimately be entitled *Corpus Mysticum Christi*. Nevertheless, although this draft was discussed by a pre-council commission, it was eventually replaced by a more juridical formulation because the members of the commission were suspicious that the "metaphor, 'Mystical Body,' did not have the clarity and exactness of thought necessary to accurately define the Church."[28] After Vatican I, "Mystical Body" ecclesiology in general, and Möhler's influence in particular began to wane under the increasingly reactionary "anti-modernist" suspicions of the prevailing Neo-Scholasticism. It would be almost fifty years before this both creative and traditional ecclesiology would be revived.

II. *Mystici Corporis Christi:*
Pope Pius XII's Encyclical on the Body of Christ

Although practically dormant after 1870, there was an astounding revival of "Mystical Body" literature beginning in 1920 and culminating with the publication in 1943 of the papal encyclical on the Feast of Saints Peter and Paul.[29] In 1942, J. J. Bluett, S.J., points out that while it would be possible to read all of the books written on this topic, the periodical literature was "vast" and international in scope. While Bluett describes the earlier literature as "doctrinal" and historical in nature, he discovers a phenomenal growth of popular

articles on the subject, especially in regard to the relationship
of this doctrine to Christian spirituality and liturgy.[30] This
suggests that at the time of the encyclical's publication the
concept of the Church as the Mystical Body of Christ was
increasingly present in both theological and pastoral spheres.
This can help to contextualize some of the arguments and
emphases of the document.

A. Central Concerns

Why the pope decided to publish a significant doctrinal
encyclical on ecclesiology in the midst of an immense war is
not clear. Although he refers to the war, he does not designate
this as the immediate impetus for the letter.[31] He describes
this statement as being prompted by two primary concerns—
one positive, the other negative. On the positive side, he is
very encouraged by three significant movements in the life of
the Church: "a renewed interest in the sacred liturgy," "the
more widely spread custom of frequent communion," and the
dynamic growth of participation of the laity, especially as it is
expressed through the work of Catholic Action.[32] This suggests
that it is primarily the new-found place of the laity, and the
theological reflection on this, that is the impetus for
re-evaluating the dominant ecclesiology.

On a more negative note, the pope wants to condemn two
errors that he sees as threatening this renewed interest in
ecclesiology. He is suspicious of what he refers to as a "false
rationalism" and of its inevitable corollary, "popular natu-
ralism," which he defines as the reduction of the mystery of
the Church to a merely juridical and social union.[33] Likewise,
he wants to reject a "false mysticism" which "attempts to elim-
inate the immovable frontier that separates creatures from
their Creator" thereby "falsifying Sacred Scripture."[34] In other
words, he is concerned about the issues that have vexed Catholic ecclesiology for over three hundred years. One is the
tendency to deny the transcendent and divine origins and tele-
ology of the Church, and to view it as only one more type of

social system existing among many in the natural realm of human existence. And the other is the Reformation dialectic regarding the visible/invisible nature of the Church, and the tendency to regard the centrality of institutional structures and hierarchical authority as auxiliary to the nature of the Church.

B. Mystical Body as the Primary Metaphor

Having pointed out from the start the absolute parameters of any renewed investigation into the reality of the Church, Pius does want to strongly endorse the metaphor of the Mystical Body of Christ and its subsequent theological implications. He devotes the entire first part of this encyclical to expounding on the appropriateness of this image to express the richness and complexity of genuine ecclesiology.

> If we would define and describe this true Church of Jesus Christ—which is the One, Holy, Catholic, Apostolic Roman Church—we shall find nothing more noble, more sublime, or more divine than the expression "the Mystical Body of Jesus Christ"—an expression which springs from and is, as it were, the fair flowering of the repeated teaching of the Sacred Scriptures and the holy Fathers.[35]

The most important aspect of the Mystical Body metaphor that emerges in the next eleven paragraphs is that it provides a way of expanding ecclesiology beyond its hierarchical, organizational, and sacramental infrastructure to include the laity, who can now be understood to occupy an "honorable, if often a lowly, place in the Christian community."[36] The Church genuinely constitutes an organically structured community of diverse but reciprocally dependent parts, which coalesce in life and action, because they are united by a single founder and endowed with his animating spirit.

This unique foundation and its subsequent source of sustenance distinguish the Church community ontologically from other merely human communities, but it nevertheless implies a fundamental similarity that cannot be denied.[37] Further on in the encyclical the distinctions are enunciated between a merely physical body, a merely moral body, and the Mystical Body.[38] In the Mystical Body, each member's individuality and freedom of will and conscience are maintained, even in their unity. Individuals are not merely subsumed in the whole but, on the contrary, the Church exists for the good of its individual members. The critical distinction between the Mystical Body and other forms of moral bodies is the existence in the former of an "internal principle," namely, the Holy Spirit, who vivifies it with a genuine unity of life and thought and raises its purpose to that of its divine source. The source of unity and common action for merely moral bodies remains the common ends for which they are organized. The pope concludes that this implies that the Church exists as a community, a socially structured body, in only an analogous sense to other types of bodies/communities we experience.

C. New Questions

This new emphasis does raise two questions previously presumed but not explicitly elucidated for ecclesiology: Who are the members of this community? And what is its relationship to the historical person of Jesus of Nazareth and the risen Christ?

1. Membership in the Church of Christ

In response to the first question, Pius insists unequivocally that

> only those are to be included as members of the Church who have been baptized and profess the true faith, and who have not been so unfortunate as to separate themselves from the unity of the Body, or

been excluded by legitimate authority. . . . It follows
that those who are divided in faith and government
cannot be living in the unity of such a Body, nor can
they be living the life of its one Divine Spirit.[39]

Unsurprisingly, Pius identifies the Mystical Body of Christ
solely with the Roman Catholic Church and those who are
juridically members of it. This excludes other Christian
communities from participating in the Church of Christ, both
as communities and, seemingly, as individuals. At the same
time, however, Pius makes two very interesting and suggestive
points. First of all, sinners are not, simply by virtue of their
sins, cut off from unity with the Church. The membership of
the Church is constituted by sinners in need of redemption
through Christ and the action of his Church.[40] Secondly, Pius
implies that those who are not explicitly united to the Church
or divided from her through schism are still somehow related
or ordered to the Mystical Body through the mercy of Christ
and the work of the Spirit.[41] He does not elaborate on this
point, but implies that there are degrees or orders of relating to
Christ that remain open beyond the explicitly visible boundaries of Roman Catholicism.

2. The Relationship of Jesus Christ to the Church: "Another Christ"

In response to the second question as to the precise relationship of the Church to Christ, Pius makes two distinctions.
First, he reasserts the traditional formula that Christ is the
"head" of the Church and, therefore, rules and guides the
Church directly. Nevertheless, because the risen Christ
remains invisible, he chooses to rule directly through his
visible vicar, the successor to Peter. For Pius, this actually
implies "that Christ and His Vicar constitute one only
Head."[42] This, in turn implies that local churches under their
respective bishops, although individual and autonomous in
some sense, ultimately derive their authority and authenticity
from the Roman Pontiff.[43] In this sense, each bishop and,
hence, each local ecclesial community, is subordinate to and

dependent on the universal Church and her head, the pope united with Jesus Christ. The relationship of the laity to Christ is similarly derived from and mediated by the "Supreme Pontiff."[44] The laity are called to share in and support the mission and ministry of the pope and thereby cooperate as genuine associates with Christ's own work of redemption.

Although the powers and authority of the whole Church derive from the single source—the Vicar of Christ—it nevertheless means that the whole Church relates to Christ in a second way, namely as a continuation of the very life of Christ. Following Bellarmine, Pius asserts that

> this appellation of the Body of Christ is not to be explained solely by the fact that Christ must be called the Head of His Mystical Body, but also by the fact that He so sustains the Church, and so in a certain sense lives in the Church, that she is, as it were, another Christ.[45]

This allows Pius to refer later in the document to the "one new man" constituted by the union of Christ with the whole Church through the intercession and communication of gifts by the Holy Spirit.[46] This indwelling of the Holy Spirit suggests that the Church as a whole can be likened analogously to the sacrament of the eucharist: we are literally transformed into that which we signify.[47] This, in turn, reminds us that while the Church is a society constituted by juridical and visible bonds, it must also be a genuine communion of love, for it is love that most efficaciously binds us to Christ and imitates him in a literal and concrete way.[48]

D. The Impact on Theology

1. Renewed Investigation of Ecclesiology

The encyclical *Mystici Corporis Christi* holds a special place in the development of ecclesiology for three reasons. First, although it stays strictly within the boundaries set by the preceding three hundred years of theological polemics, it does set the stage for a vast expansion and renewed investigation of ecclesiology in general. By sanctioning a fruitful new metaphor as the starting point of ecclesiological reflection, this encyclical opens the door (perhaps unwittingly) to a recovery of biblical, patristic and medieval sources for this terminology as well as to new modes of interpretation.

2. Recovery of the Communal Dimension

Secondly, in the *Mystical Body of Christ* the pope discerns a more integrative and holistic concept to challenge the wholly one-sided juridical and institutional definitions of the Church, which had not only diminished Catholic theological discourse, but also negatively impacted the inner life and vitality of the Church itself. He reminds the Church that there are *two* vital aspects essential to her salvific mission: a community of faithful people bound together in love *and* a visible institution that acts concretely in union with Christ and his Holy Spirit to bring about God's plan of salvation.

3. New Dynamic Metaphor

Finally, while this encyclical clearly means to keep ecclesiological discourse within a clearly proscribed arena, it actually introduces a dynamic, organic, and open-ended analogy, which evokes multiple interpretations. In the years after its publication, this encyclical would spawn a great deal of ecumenical and interdisciplinary dialogue, as well as challenge the assumptions of absolute papal hegemony and the primacy of the external visible dimensions of ecclesiology and their Christological foundations. As the terminology of "communion" began to supplant that of "society" (although used interchangeably by Pius XII), the ramifications for practical and basic issues of the Church's internal and external relationships were significant at many levels.

4. Limitations

While representing a great step forward in theology, fundamental limitations in understanding the Church and serious obstacles for greater unity remain in the wake of this document. Because it exclusively identifies the Mystical Body of Christ with the Roman Catholic Church, the document fails to offer a legitimate inclusion of all the baptized into the Body of Christ. Furthermore, by failing to seriously address the ecclesial and spiritual status of the non-baptized and the presence of grace in other religious traditions, it misses an opportunity to reflect on the deeper and more profound implications of this biblical metaphor. Pius XII also fails to move beyond the overly juridical and hierarchical understanding of the Church that developed in the centuries after the Counter-Reformation. His "top-down" ecclesiology tends to diminish the significant possibilities for a broader interpretation present in the Pauline theology of the Church. The radical communal and egalitarian dimensions of the Pauline version are not given an adequate presentation in this document. Finally, the question of the full inclusion and participation of the laity in the life of the Church remains under-developed and insufficiently articulated in this encyclical.

Nevertheless, this document represents a fundamental shift and a significant new beginning for theological reflection on the Church.

III. The Ecclesiology of Yves Congar, O.P.

Yves Congar claims that his life's ambition, conceived while he was still a student in the late 1920's, had always been to write a full treatise on the Church.[49] Later in his life, while he realized that he would never fully accomplish that task, he described his many written works as "fragments" of that immense project. His research and writing on ecclesiology and related issues spanned more than fifty years, and the American

Catholic theologian Richard McBrien has named him the most influential theologian of Vatican II as well as "the most distinguished ecclesiologist of this century and perhaps the post-Tridentine era."[50] Under the tutelage of his most famous teacher, M. D. Chenu, O.P., and other Dominican theologians, Congar became deeply engaged in what was known as the *ressourcement* (the return to the sources). This movement focused on recovering and culling the primary sources of the Christian tradition, particularly texts from the patristic and medieval periods. Congar immersed himself in the biblical, patristic, and medieval sources of theology which, eventually, expanded and challenged the reigning Neo-Scholasticism of his day. Chenu also introduced him to the work of Möhler, who quickly became "a source, *the* source" he needed to inspire him to begin a serious and new approach to ecclesiology.[51] Perhaps his earliest significant contribution to theology was his founding of the series *Unam Sanctum* in 1935, which tried to "recover for ecclesiology the inspiration and the resources of an older and deeper Tradition."[52] Very early in this collection he included a translation of Möhler's work *The Unity of the Church*. This set the tone not only for the rest of the series but for Congar's own work. He, like Möhler, wanted to develop a vision of the Church that was more vital, synthetic, communal and pneumatologically based. Unlike Möhler, and most theologians of his own day, he also saw the need for an ecclesiology that not only included other Christian denominations but also understood the "realism of grace and the Word" in cultures and peoples in general.[53]

It was from this twin starting point of recovering the tradition and pointing toward a new future that Congar produced his most influential pre-Vatican II articles and books. While at least four of his major works during this period had a profound and lasting impact on theologians and the Church as a whole, I will concentrate on the two that most systematically and directly outlined Congar's interpretation of the Mystical Body of Christ ecclesiology and his early understanding of communion and community: *Lay People in the Church* and *The Mystery of the Church.*[54] These two works differ widely in both method and scope. *The Mystery of the Church* is actually a collection of essays, many originally written in the late 1930's and again in the late 1940's (at which time he was a prisoner of war for five years). It serves as a catechesis on Pentecost given to lay pilgrims, which in many ways summarizes the early studies of the sources and issues that will coalesce in his more thorough and systematic book, *Lay People in the Church*.

Lay People in the Church was Congar's first major attempt to develop a systematic ecclesiology from a new and revolutionary point of view. While he will revise this ecclesiology in the light of Vatican II and insights he develops later in his career,[55] this text had a profound impact on the major documents of Vatican II and the main lines of what would develop into "communion ecclesiology."

In the *Mystery of the Church,* Congar notes that it is his understanding of revelation that unites and directs his reflections. In this light, a sincere evaluation of the past must go hand-in-hand with an ongoing analysis of the life of the Church as it is understood from within. He arrives at the conclusion that pneumatology acts as the basis for ecclesiology. It best explains the essentially Trinitarian plan for the Church: the economy of the divine life itself. It is the Spirit that makes Jesus' life and message continually present by enlivening and animating the emerging and ongoing life of the Christian community. Because of the unique nature of this community, this social unit, Congar deemed that the term "communion" most adequately describes it. A communion is a free union of individual persons united not only "horizontally" through interpersonal bonds but also "vertically" by their common relationship to God through Christ in the Spirit. The Spirit, who genuinely unites one free person to another through a unique bond of love and communion, therefore, exists as a concrete living and historically acting reality. Through Aquinas, Congar was encouraged to think of the Church as a complex communion of persons, united in the

Spirit, who literally "extend" the presence of Christ and his mission in history.

Central to this unique type of community is what Congar refers to as the "hierarchical function or principle." It bears the responsibility of teaching, spiritual governance, and mediating the prayer of the community. The hierarchical element always functions as a service and a servant to the wider communion. At the same time, he realizes that the hierarchical principle is balanced by a "communal principle." This principle or function includes the body of all the faithful who have been baptized and are thereby fully part of the saving plan of God in Christ. Congar realizes the need to redirect ecclesiology, and he develops what he calls a "laicology." In *Lay People in the Church*, he systematically investigates ecclesiology by starting on the other side—the communal and lay side—of the ecclesial dialectic. While he still maintains a somewhat "top-down" ecclesiology, he stresses that both functions—the hierarchical and the communal—are foundational principles and that the latter could bear the greatest fruit, thus deserving further investigation and development.

Congar carefully balanced this model by insisting that Christ and his Holy Spirit relate fully, if somewhat differently, to both dimensions of the Church. The laity cannot be reduced, therefore, to being mere subjects of the hierarchy, because both act as true means and sources of sanctification in and for the world. All of the faithful are the Church in a completely literal sense—no member is more part or essential to the Mystical Body of Christ than another. Congar insists upon the significant unity and continuity between the Church and the world, and he understands the sanctifying power of the Church as acting within the world and upon the world primarily through the laity.

In this context, Congar feels confident in describing the Church as a "sacrament" of Christ, most clearly represented in the eucharist, where the real union between the triune God and the life of the community is made manifest and visible. This communion constitutes the Church in its very essence and represents both its reality and mission. Nevertheless, to meet the vital needs of the day, Congar believes that theology needs to be transformed further by reconnecting it more fully with the Tradition and the growing insights of the modern world. The Church itself has to continually respond to the current needs and insights of cultures and contexts by creatively drawing from its vast wells of Tradition and traditions.

IV. Toward a Deeper Ecclesiology on the Eve of Vatican II: *The Church is a Communion* by Jerome Hamer, O.P.[56]

Written after the Second Vatican Council had been called and published almost simultaneously with its opening, Jerome Hamer's work, *The Church is a Communion*, had a direct and significant impact on the Council. The documents clearly reflect his influence. Jerome Hamer, O.P., a student of Congar and other prominent Dominican scholars, was a young, yet leading professor of theology in Rome at the beginning of the Second Vatican Council. Hamer's project was not particularly original in that he mainly drew together and synthesized the tremendous amount of ecclesiological reflection that had developed in the two decades after the publication of *Mystici Corporis Christi*. Hamer organized his work, however, in a way that made it immediately accessible to most of the theological and clerical community in the Roman Catholic Church. He laid the material out in practically a "manualist" format—making proper distinctions and definitions in response to a systematic series of questions on the nature and functions of the Church. This format, familiar to most people trained in the pre-conciliar Church, summarized the developments in systematic theology (especially the work of Bouyer, Chenu, Congar, de Lubac and Rahner) and combined these with developments in scriptural research (particularly of the

Dominican Benoit) and the historical recovery of the patristic and medieval sources.

By drawing together the many diverse but converging streams of ecclesiology emerging in the twenty years after the publication of *Mystici Corporis Christi*, Hamer outlined and clarified many of the intriguing new insights of the pre-conciliar period. What distinguishes Hamer's project, however, is his systematically investigating and grounding the Church as a "communion." He concludes that the concept of communion functions as the necessary starting point for a renewed definition of the nature of the Church.

Hamer thus articulates succinctly the work begun by Möhler. The dynamic term of "communion" enables theologians to envision a new fundamental relationship between the communal and hierarchical dimensions of the Church. Communion proves to be as helpful a concept in expressing the relationship between the various parts and the whole, as it is in describing oneness to something so demographically and geographically complex as the international Church. Because every individual member, and each distinct community, shares in the same Head (Christ), the same Soul (the Holy Spirit), and the same institutional structures (scripture, sacraments, doctrine, hierarchical authority), all can be truly described as a "single numerical whole."[57] Communion implies that these various aspects of life we share in are not merely external but mediate a more direct and intimate "whole" that constitutes the very nature of the Church. That we remain "one" though "many" becomes the fundamental state of our lives and primary determinate of our actions. This reality depends on the belief that the same Holy Spirit dwells in each individual member, simultaneously giving each the necessary gifts to maintain both the external life of the community and the eternal bond of love. For this reason, Hamer advocates further study of the intimate connection between pneumatology and ecclesiology. Working out more clearly the relationship between the Spirit and the Church will vivify and enhance any understanding of the genuine unity of the Church.[58]

For Hamer, the term "communion" best expresses the relationship between these two foundational realities. Like
Congar, he recognizes that communion represents the bond of
love between both the individual members and the integral
unity of the whole body with the life of God. Hamer also
believes that communion resolves any confusion between the
interrelationship of "the one and the many" by offering a
comprehensive vision of how a genuine unity among many
diverse parts remains feasible in the actual life of the community. He concludes his analysis by observing the need for a
greater reflection on, and penetration of, the mystery of the
Holy Spirit and its dynamic unifying and coordinating activity
both within the Church and within the Godhead itself.

Notes

1. Augustine, *The City of God* (*De Civitate Dei*), trans. by Marcus Dods (Grand Rapids, Michigan: Eerdman's Publishing Co., 1993).
2. Augustine, *City of God*, bk. 25, ch. 26, pp. 306-307.
3. *Mystici Corporis Christi* (MCC), p. 10.
4. Yves Congar, O.P., *Lay People in the Church*, trans. Donald Attwater, rev. ed. (Maryland: The Newman Press, 1965); see particularly pp. 38–54.
5. Louis Bouyer, *The Church of God: Body of Christ and Temple of the Spirit*, trans. Charles Underhill Quinn (Chicago: Franciscan Herald Press, 1982) 3–145.
6. Ibid., pp. 77–81. *Jansenism* was a movement begun at Lovain by Carmelius Jansen (d. 1638) that held that through Original Sin human beings lost not only supernatural grace but were totally corrupted in their natural human condition as well. This meant that anything purely natural was evil, and that the possibility of redemption and salvation was limited and narrow. This lead to a very strong theory of predestination and a morally rigorous style of Christian life. It was seen to contradict the great Medieval synthesis of the Thomists and to reinforce the theological claims of Protestantism.
   Gallicanism appeared after Rome condemned Jansenism because of its widespread popularity among the French clergy. (Hence, the name derives from its French, or Gallic, origins.) In 1682, the French clergy declared that the pope had only spiritual authority, in keeping with the council of Constance, and that his pronouncements had to be approved of by a council representing the whole Church. This claim was explicitly condemned at Vatican I. *Febronianism or Josephism* (named after the emperor Joseph II, d. 1790) was the name given to a variety of Gallicanism transplanted to Germany in the eighteenth century. The Church there also began to insist that the pope's juridical powers were limited and that his decisions on all doctrinal matters had to be ratified by a representative council of the whole Church. For more information see McBrien, Richard, *Catholicism* (San Francisco: Harper, 1994) pp. 636-649.
7. Congar, *Lay People in the Church*, 44–46.
8. Ibid. See also Bouyer, 74–76, and Henri de Lubac, S.J., *The Splendor of the Church*, trans. Michael Mason (New Jersey: Paulist Press, 1963) 51–56. The classic text by Robert

Bellarmine is *De controversiis christianae fidae*, in *Opera omnia*, 12 vols., ed. Justinus Fevre (Paris: L. Vives, 1870–1874); see principally vols. 2 and 5.

9. Congar, *Lay People in the Church*, 45.

10. See particularly, Patrick Granfield, "The Church as 'Societas Perfecta' in the Schemata of Vatican I," *Church History*, 48 (December, 1979) 431–446; and "The Rise and Fall of Societas Perfecta," *Concilium No. 157: May Church Minister's Be Politicians?*, eds. Peter Huizing and Knewt Walf (New York: Seabury, 1982) 3-4.

11. Granfield, "The Rise and Fall of 'Societas Perfecta,'" 3.

12. Ibid.

13. Ibid. Granfield believes that the term in its new form probably originated with the Austrian canonist Franciscus Rautenstrauch (d.1785) but that it was quickly embraced by canonists in the following century, and in papal documents, beginning with Pius IX in 1839 (p. 5).

14. Granfield, "The Church as Societas Perfecta," 432ff. Although these two schemata or drafts are not official conciliar statements, they were offered to the bishops for discussion and debate. The first draft, "Supremis pastoris," received considerable attention, but was eventually revised by the German theologian Joseph Kleutgen, S.J., as "Tametsi Deus." While neither draft was ever voted on by the council fathers and so cannot be considered official Church documents, Granfield, Bouyer and other experts believe they represent the dominant strain of nineteenth century ecclesiology.

15. Ibid., 436; Granfield takes these and the following quotes from J. D. Mansi in, *Sacrorum conciliorum nova et aplissima collectio*, 53 vols. (Paris and Leipzig: 1901–1927), 51:863–916. Hereafter referred to as Mansi. This quote is from Mansi, 51:540.

16. Ibid., Granfield, 444, from Mansi 53:315.

17. Granfield, 441. Granfield points out that the theme of the Church as a perfect society appears in the encyclicals *Immortale Dei* (1885), *Sapientiae Christianae* (1890), *Satis Cognitum* (1896) of Leo XIII and in MCC (1943) and *Mediator Dei* (1947) of Pius XII. For the exact references see the English translation of these texts entitled: *The Church Teaches: Documents of the Church in English Translation*, ed. and trans. by J.F. Clarkson et al. (St. Louis: Herder Book Co., 1955) 86–121. Likewise, this terminology appears in almost every theological manual and catechism composed during this period.

18. See particularly, Gerald A. McCool, *Nineteenth–Century Scholasticism: The Search for a Unitary Method* (New York: Fordham University Press, 1989). O'Meara, Thomas F. "Aquinas' Theology and Modernity." Proceedings of the Aquinas Symposium, April, 1988, pp. 1–23.

19. This terminology was introduced and defended at Vatican II (by Karol Wojtyla, the Bishop of Krakow, among others) but was dismissed in favor of more integrative and biblical metaphors, as will be discussed later.

20. Thomas F. O'Meara, O.P., "Revelation and History: Schelling, Möhler and Congar," *The Irish Theological Quarterly*, 53:1 (1987) 26; for a more thorough analysis of the influence of romantic-idealism on German Catholic theology and its subsequent development see also Thomas O'Meara's *Romantic Idealism and Roman Catholicism: Schelling and the Theologians* (Notre Dame: Notre Dame University Press, 1982).

21. Bouyer, 91–93.

22. J. A. Möhler, *Die Einheit in der Kirche* (Cologne and Olten: Hegner, 1956), originally published in 1825.

23. Bouyer, 93–94.

24. Ibid., 95.

25. Ibid., 94–104.

26. The title of the final text was *Symbolik* in German, the English translation *Symbolism: The Doctrinal Differences between Protestants and Catholics*, trans. J. B. Robinson (London: Gibbings & Co., 1894).

27. Ibid., 104; Hamer, 15.

28. Hamer, 15–17.

29. Joseph J. Bluett, S.J., "Current Theology: The Mystical Body of Christ: 1890–1940" in *Theological Studies*, 3 (1942) 260–289.

30. Ibid., 262.

31. MCC, para. 4. It would seem from our vantage point that World War II challenged many of the presumptions of not only ecclesiology but Christianity. The fact that the Church (both Roman Catholic and Christian) was at war with itself seems to practically and concretely contradict not only the unity of the Church but its self-understanding as somehow a continuation of the work of Christ. But Pius XII chose not to dwell on these issues, although they perhaps underlie the "urgency" with which he begins the letter.

32. MCC, 8.

33. MCC, 9.

34. Ibid.

35. MCC, 13.

36. MCC, 17.

37. MCC, 25ff.

38. MCC, 61–63.

39. MCC, 22; see also MCC, 41.

40. MCC, 23–24.

41. MCC, 102–103.

42. MCC, 40.

43. MCC, 42.

44. MCC, 44.

45. MCC, 53.

46. MCC, 77.

47. MCC, 81–84.

48. MCC, 72–74.

49. Yves Congar, O.P., "My Path-findings in the Theology of Laity and Ministries," in *The Jurist* 32 (1972), no. 2, 169–188.

50. Richard McBrien, "Church and Ministry: The Achievement of Yves Congar," *Theological Digest* 32 (1985) 203.

51. O'Meara, "Revelation and History," 29.

52. Congar, "Path-findings ... ," 170.

53. Ibid., 172.

54. *The Mystery of the Church*, trans. A.V. Littledale (Baltimore: Helicon Press, 1960) was originally published in French as two separate books: *Esquisses du mystere de l'Eglise* and *La Pentecote: Chartres, 1956* (Paris: Editions du Cerf, 1956). *Lay People in the Church: A Study for a Theology of the Laity*, trans. Donald Attwater (Westminster, Maryland: The Newman Press, 1965), originally published in French as *Jalons pour une theologie du laicat* (Paris: Les Editions du Cerf, 1957). His two other most important works from this period are: *Divided Christendom: A Catholic Study of the Problem of Reunion* (London: G. Bles, 1939), and *Tradition and Traditions*, trans. M. Naseby and T. Rainvorough (New York: Macmillan, 1967), originally published in French as *La tradition et traditions*, 2 vols. (Paris: Librarie Artheme Fayard, 1960, 1963); for a fuller analysis of the ecclesiology of Congar see Timothy MacDonald, *The Ecclesiology of Yves Congar: Foundational Themes* (Lanham, MD: University Press of America, 1984).

55. I will address some of these insights and revisions in the fourth chapter of this book.

56. Jerome Hamer, *The Church is a Communion*, trans. Ronald Matthews (New York: Sheed and Ward, 1964); originally published in French under the title, *L'Eglise est une communion* (Paris: Les Editions du Cerf, 1962).

57. Ibid., 182.

58. Ibid., 187.

Chapter 2

The Ecclesiology of the Constitutions on the Church

I. An Ecclesiology Out of the Documents

The Second Vatican Council cannot be understood without a thorough study of the documents that emerged from it. This chapter is intended as an introduction to and "walk" through the major documents. I will attempt to point out dominant themes, unifying motifs, new insights, fundamental principles, as well as inconsistencies, significant problems, and new syntheses that arise throughout the major conciliar texts. As such it is both a summary and analysis of the Council itself, and I am convinced that an evolving but consistent ecclesiological vision unites all of the documents. No summary, however, can replace the reading and reflecting on the documents themselves—they express the faith and thinking of the whole Church. This book can only serve as a guide through the texts as it attempts to shed light on the complexities of such a large body of thought.

Although primarily focusing on a detailed analysis of the major documents devoted to the Constitution on the Church (*Lumen Gentium* and *Gaudium et Spes*), I shall begin by briefly examining the first significant constitutional document produced by the Council: *Sacrosanctum Concilium*.[1] I will also note some clarifications made in later explanatory documents connected with this text. In addition to my analysis of the major constitutional documents, I will describe and interpret some related declarations made by the Council, particularly

those pertaining to ecumenism, the nature and role of the episcopacy, the role of the laity, and the exercise of religious
liberty. These various decrees and declarations advance and
expand many of the nascent insights of *Lumen Gentium*, and
also provide a kind of bridge between the Dogmatic and
Pastoral Constitutions on the Church. I shall conclude the
chapter with a discussion of those aspects of ecclesiology that
emerged or were clarified by the Council, and shall suggest an
overall schema for interpreting the ecclesiology of the Council.

II. Sacrosanctum Concilium

At the outset of the Council, the council fathers were
presented with a number of "Preparatory Schema" on an array
of issues. That the bishops chose by and large to abandon the
prepared agenda and strike out on their own stands as one of
the most intriguing aspects of the Council.[2] In fact, while
many different texts were available to work on simultaneously, the council fathers chose to take up the constitution
on the liturgy as their first order of business. (This text stands
in fact as the only constitutional document promulgated
during the first session of the Council.) Following the trajectory of the theological firmament in the twenty years after the
promulgation of *Mystici Corporis Christi,* the Council proposed
to "impart an ever-increasing vigor to the Christian life of the
faithful . . . [and] to foster whatever can promote union among
all who believe in Christ," as well as, "strengthen whatever can
help to call all mankind into the Church's fold" (SC, 1). The
council fathers determined that the reform and promotion of
the liturgy constituted the first step in a general renewal of
both the internal life of the Church and its external structural
presence and mission in the world.

The influence of the theological currents discussed in the
previous chapter emerge almost immediately in the document. The second paragraph concentrates on how the liturgy,
especially the eucharist, manifests the invisible, divine

elements of the mystery of Christ as well as the Church and its visible, human, "worldly" dimensions. It describes the Church as a "pilgrim": a human reality endowed with and directed toward the divine, where action moves toward contemplation, the visible toward the invisible. The liturgy both expresses the presence of the Spirit and "builds up" that presence in the lives of the faithful and the Church as a whole. It increases the power of the Church to preach Christ and to act as an efficacious sign of his presence and his desire to gather all people, both those "inside and outside" the Church, into a single people or "fold."

The significance of this introduction lies in two presumptions that I see operating underneath it. First, the emphasis on the liturgy, and particularly the eucharist, presupposes an integral and essential unity between the visible, structural, and hierarchical elements of the Church and its invisible and interpersonal/communal dimensions. Secondly, the terms "pilgrim," "sign," and "preacher" presuppose a sacramental understanding of the Church. The liturgical life of the Church expresses not just a concern with the internal and "vertical" life of the community but also its external mission to the wider human community as an instrument and source of conversion and unity. From the beginning, structural and institutional cohesion are subordinated to mission. The council fathers chose to contextualize the reform and adaptation of the liturgy—a seemingly internal and institutional concern—within the scope of the Church's wider nature and mission to serve as an instrument of the Spirit to both the Church and the world.

As the first written document, the ecclesiological principles underlying it remain somewhat nascent. Nevertheless, one can discern a clear dependence on the metaphor of the Mystical Body of Christ and its attendant ecclesiology in the introductory chapters. This ecclesiology manifests itself most clearly once the text starts to articulate concrete norms for the reform of the liturgy.[3] The document states that these norms should serve to enable the Christian people to understand the liturgies with ease and to "take part in them fully, actively and as a community" (SC, 21). Echoing the dual foci of ecclesiology proposed by Congar and Hamer, "the Hierarchic and Communal Nature of the liturgy"(SC, 25) should evoke these norms. While the rights of legitimate authority and the power proper to ordained offices in the Church maintain their importance, the document clarifies, with some vigor, that equal weight must be paid to active and heart-felt participation of all the faithful in each liturgy. Furthermore, the text continually emphasizes that the public, communal, and unifying characteristics of the liturgical celebrations disclose the fullest essence of the life of the Church.[4]

Most post-Vatican II appraisals of this Constitution emphasize its failure to give a "sustained theological perspective and enunciated vision," and therefore the body of the document remains "sketchy" and "weak," particularly when compared to *Lumen Gentium*.[5] Nevertheless, given its early completion and the greater inclusion of the broader ecclesiology articulated at the Council in the post-conciliar decrees related to this document,[6] the liturgical reform inaugurated here concretely embodies many of the fruits of the pre-conciliar theological reflection on the nature of the Church as a communion. The absence of a fully articulated pneumatology and, hence, a thoughtful and systematic understanding of the Trinity and its life in mission, however, strikes me as the most significant and glaring weakness in the documents and discussions emerging from the first session of the Council.

III. Lumen Gentium

The council fathers discussed the Dogmatic Constitution on the Church, *Lumen Gentium*, over three sessions of the Council—from the opening session in 1962 through the middle of the third session in 1964. After passing through numerous revisions, and considering thousands of amendments, the final text was approved at the end of the third session (November 21, 1964) by a vote of 2151 to 5.[7] In promulgating this document, Pope Paul VI stated:

> Henceforth it will be possible to have a fuller understanding of the thought of God in relation to the Mystical Body of Christ, and we shall be able to draw therefrom clearer and surer norms for the life of the Church, greater strength in order to lead men to salvation, better hopes for the reign of Christ in the world.[8]

This speech marked the culmination and triumph of the ecclesiology of the Mystical Body—from its nineteenth century revival by Johann Möhler through its seeming displacement at Vatican I and, finally, its full integration into the constitutional definition of the doctrine of the Church at Vatican II.

While *Lumen Gentium* did not officially contradict previous ecclesiological syntheses (the council fathers in fact took great pains to insist on its continuity with the tradition, particularly with the thought of Vatican I), it certainly redirected Roman Catholic ecclesiology in a creatively new way. An outline of the chapters of the document itself betrays a dramatic and paradigmatic shift from the official ecclesiologies promulgated by the post-Tridentine magisterium. The successive chapter titles are "The Mystery of the Church," "The People of God," "The Church is Hierarchical," "The Laity," "The Call to Holiness," "Religious," "The Pilgrim Church," and "Our Lady." I believe that the change of emphasis evident in the ordering of the chapters belies an even deeper transformation in the speculative and practical theological moorings of the Church's self-understanding. Not only the title but also the second sentence of the first chapter discloses the scope and orientation of the whole document: "The Church, in Christ, is in the nature of a sacrament—a sign and instrument, that is, of communion with God and of unity among all men" (LG, 1).

Chapter 1: The Mystery of the Church

Contrasting with most previous treatises on the Church, the Council chose to begin its examination of the Church's nature and mission by reflecting on the mystery of God and God's gratuitous choice to share the divine life with humanity. The Council grounds ecclesiology in the triune life of God and the missions of the persons of the Trinity toward creation. Furthermore, because this mystery of the Trinity and its plan for the world can only be known through revelation, any ecclesiology must be thoroughly rooted in scripture as its foundational source and the test of its authenticity. These two insights set the pattern for this chapter, which itself acts as an overview of the whole document.

The second, third and fourth paragraphs of the text systematically lay the triune plan of creation and redemption as narrated in both testaments of scripture. It explains the creation by the Father, redemption through the Son's obedience to the Father's will, and the empowering of a visible community by the Holy Spirit.

The triune life of God and God's reign, therefore, serve as the context for any discussion of the nature of the Church itself. This implies that the Church cannot be understood or examined apart from the action of Jesus Christ, who founded it, and the ongoing activity of the Spirit, who unites and directs its life. In paragraph 5, the document places the "founding" of the Church in Jesus' preaching of the Good News. From Jesus Christ the Church receives its mission "of proclaiming and establishing among all peoples the kingdom of Christ and of God, and she is, on earth, the seed and beginning of that kingdom" (LG, 5).

Having determined the fundamental nature and mission of the Church, in the sixth paragraph the document turns to the scriptures to call to mind a variety of images that expand and elaborate on this basic understanding of the Church. The text describes the Church variously as a "gateway" to Christ; as God's "fold"; as a "cultivated field" and a "choice vineyard"; as "the building of God," "the temple of the Lord" and a "holy city"; as "our mother," a "spotless spouse" and the "Spouse of Christ"; and as an "exile" on a journey home (LG, 6). But, ultimately, the most suggestive and significant image presented by scripture to describe the Church remains "the Body of Christ" (LG, 7).

Paragraph 7 elaborates extensively on the image of the Body of Christ. The effect of Jesus' redemptive action through his death and resurrection transforms human beings into a "new creation" (LG, 7). The communication of Christ's Spirit to the "body" of his followers acts as the primary source of this new creation.

The sacraments of the Church, particularly the eucharist, literally incorporate the members of the Church into a "communion" with Christ and with one another. The text goes on to describe this communion as one allowing for a wide diversity of both members and functions but also one where the Spirit is at work distributing and coordinating these gifts in a way that continually builds up Christ's body. The text asserts that the primacy of these gifts belongs "to the grace of the apostles to whose authority the Spirit himself subjects even those who are endowed with charisms" (LG, 7).

The Spirit gives "the body unity through himself, both by his own power and by the interior union of the members" (LG, 7). The Spirit's power to stimulate genuine love in the hearts of each member emerges as the key to this interpersonal unity between the members through and in the Spirit. Furthermore, a thorough interdependence between the members characterizes the interpersonal bond formed by the Spirit such that "if one member suffers anything, all the members suffer with him, and if one member is honored, all the members together rejoice" (1 Cor 12:26) (LG, 7). The image of the Body of Christ, therefore, functions to explain not only how the Church acts as a communion of persons that truly represents Christ in history but also how the Spirit of Christ operates as the organizing and unifying force at the heart of the Church.

Paragraph 8 takes up the issues surrounding the implications of the Church as the Mystical Body of Christ, especially in the light of other pre-conciliar interpretations of the nature of the Church. It describes the Church as a "visible society" composed of both "hierarchical organs" and a "spiritual community" (LG, 8). These two realities, though distinct, are not opposed but in fact compose "one complex reality" analogous to the mystery of the incarnate Word (LG, 8).

This new integral interpretation of the visible and invisible dimensions of the Church inevitably leads to the question of the relationship between the visible organized Roman Catholic Church and the "invisible" broader Church of Christ. All structures, even the Roman Church itself, serve the building up of the wider spiritual community referred to here as the Church of Christ.

This initial chapter ends clarifying that the Church, unlike its Head, is not "holy, innocent, and undefiled" (LG, 8). Sinners both compose the membership of the Church and act as the mediators and subjects of her efficacious action. The Church, therefore, remains simultaneously "holy and always in need of purification" and strives constantly to achieve renewal through penance and conversion (LG, 8). Far from weakening her, however, this ongoing process of conversion and renewal expresses the message the Church proclaims to the world: that all good things come through the power of the risen Lord and his sanctifying Spirit. In this way, the Church, even in its sinfulness and incompleteness, discloses the mystery of Christ, which will only be fully consummated at the end of time.

Chapter 2: The People of God

Having laid the foundation for the ecclesiological synthesis the document aims at in chapter 1, chapters 2 and 3 are constructed to examine in more detail the two realities that compose the one Church. Chapter 2, therefore, sets out to determine the nature and configuration of the wider and invisible community of Christ, enlivened and animated by his Spirit. The council fathers determined that the term "The People of God," again drawn from scripture,[9] most appropriately explains and elaborates on the reality of this spiritual community.

Critical to this choice of "The People of God" as the defining metaphor for the spiritual dimension of the Church are three primary considerations. First, the term seems to embody most fully the anthropological and theological insight necessary for the kind of ecclesial vision the document invokes. The opening lines of the chapter state that

> At all times and in every race, anyone who fears God and does what is right has been acceptable to him (cf. Acts 10:35). He has, however, willed to make men holy and save them, not as individuals without any bond or link between them, but rather to make them into a people who might acknowledge him and serve him in holiness. (LG, 9)

There is something in human nature and the plan of God itself that compels a social and communal interpretation of the human person. Human beings were created by God to be persons-in-communion, and God's salvific plan for the redemption of humanity incorporates this fact. This social context for individual salvation also offers an alternative approach to the many prevailing individualistic pieties and ideologies present in modern Western cultures.

The second advantage of this terminology, I believe, lies in its ability to incorporate both testaments of scripture. It clarifies both the continuity and discontinuity between "the Israelite race" as God's chosen people and subjects of the first covenant, and the people of the new covenant established by the life and mission of Jesus Christ (LG, 9).[10] This accentuates God's ongoing presence in history, as well as God's definite choice to reveal himself through a concrete, visible, and historically contingent group of people. It was only such a community of people who could truly reveal God's universal saving will: "[God] called a race made up of Jews and Gentiles which would be one, not according to the flesh, but in the Spirit, and this race would be the new People of God" (LG, 9). The metaphor of "The People of God," therefore, potentially illustrates the diverse and universal scope of the spiritual community. It implies a community where the Spirit acts in utter freedom to draw people of every race and time and culture into the Body of Christ, not only *undeterred* by limitations of historical contingency, but *through* them.

The foregoing suggests the third motive I discern for choosing this terminology, evident in the opening section of the chapter. Because the new people of God have Christ as their head and his Spirit as their soul, they in turn take on the messianic and evangelical character of his mission and message. "The People of God," therefore, describes a community of people who can truly act as a "visible sacrament" of the saving unity that God wills for all humanity. This unity of people manifests itself directly in human history "though it transcends at once all times and all racial boundaries" (LG, 9). "The People of God" serves as a rich metaphor for the universal and sacramental character of the Church's communal and "spiritual" dimension. It allows the Church of Christ to be described in a wider scope than the narrow confines of a particular institutional structure, while at the same time insuring that this community has a concrete and historical character that protects it from becoming a merely intangible and ahistorical conception.

The sacramental connotations of the metaphor "The People of God" also suggests how the community shares in the threefold office of Jesus Christ: priest, prophet and king. Paragraphs 10 through 13 probe how the Church shares in these three characteristics of Christ. The text begins by distinguishing between the sacramental and "hierarchical" priesthood and the common priesthood of all the baptized. The ministerial priesthood acts to "form" and "rule" the community and particularly to express "the person of Christ" through the liturgy, which the priest offers to God in the "name of the people" (LG, 10). The community, for its part, shares in the priesthood of Christ through "participation" in the eucharist, prayer, and common life of the Church as well as through daily "witness" and acts of charity and the other virtues (LG, 10). Both dimensions of the one priesthood of Jesus Christ, however, are ordered to the same common end: to bring into "operation" the "sacred nature and organic structure" of the community (LG, 11). This implies that there exists a fundamental unity of life that underlies the community and toward which both its liturgical/sacramental and moral activity tend.

While the eucharist remains the "source and summit" of all liturgical and moral activity, the common priesthood implies that all of the individual and concrete sacramental and moral actions of the Church and its members take place within a communal context. The text cites Christian marriage as the greatest example of this reality. The Christian family literally acts as a "domestic Church" and signifies in an intense way the very mystery of the Church. Marriage and family life serve to ground and provide the conditions of life necessary for the growth in sanctity and perfection characteristic of both dimensions of the priesthood. In this sense, the text suggests that the family, as the first and most basic experience of Christian community, operates as the literal source of all the other larger units and functions (states of life) that coalesce into the one community or people of God.

Paragraph 12 explores the way in which the people of God participate in Christ's prophetic office. The possession of the truth in the manner of genuinely acting as both the recipient and witness of the word of God marks the most distinctive way in which the Church demonstrates its prophetic function. The Church acts prophetically first of all through its unanimity of faith as expressed in its consensus in regard to doctrine. She also acts prophetically through the unity she demonstrates in her concrete life of mutual service and interdependence. The distribution and coordination of various gifts or charisms by the Holy Spirit enables this genuine unity of life. All of these gifts, from the most remarkable to the most ordinary, work toward the "renewal and building up of the Church" (LG, 12). United in love and animated by the mutual sharing of the charisms of the Spirit, the Christian community transcends the ordinary expectations of a functional association of people, united in achieving a common goal, by manifesting an extraordinary and providential presence of God's own life and word.

The text then turns its attention to the "kingship" of the people of God. Kingship here is generally equated with the universal nature and mission of the Church.

> Since the Kingdom of Christ is not of this world . . . the Church or People of God which establishes this kingdom does not take away anything from the temporal welfare of any people. Rather she fosters and takes to herself, insofar as they are good, the abilities, the resources and customs of people. In so taking them to herself she purifies, strengthens and elevates them. (LG, 13)

Two very important theological principles flow from this profound insight.

Firstly, after the Council, this and similar statements would become the basis of what can be termed the "inculturation mandate" of the Council, namely that the Church exists primarily to incarnate herself in each distinct culture in ways that both affirm and challenge the basic structures and foundations of that culture. Drawing the older tradition of "grace building on and perfecting nature," the mission of the Church can be described as developing and perfecting the reality of grace already present in creation through the diversity of cultures she engages. This mission presumes that the Spirit is already present and working in peoples and cultures before the explicit arrival and activity of the Church. It affirms God's kingship over all creation, even that not explicitly Christian.

Secondly, it devolves upon the Catholic Church, from this principle of pneumatological universality, to act as the explicit agent seeking "to return all humanity and all its goods under Christ the Head in the unity of his Spirit" (LG, 13). The Catholic Church as the concrete embodiment of the people of God efficaciously promotes the "fullness of unity" required by the divine plan for the world. As such, the Church itself represents the possibility of this unity by acting as a sign of the type of unity it seeks. The text characterizes this unity as one made up of very many diverse parts, a diversity due to the great variety of "ranks," "duties" and conditions or states of life among the members of the visible community (LG, 13). This unity can also be attributed to communion of various communities or particular churches that retain distinct traditions while at the same time sharing a basic unity of life around the "chair of Peter" and the "assembly of charity" (LG, 13).

From here it moves to the pneumatological principle of universality. This notion of the universality of the people of God, and particularly the assumption of God's universal saving will for all humanity, does raise the question of the role and necessity of the Church to bring about this salvation and to the various degrees of relationship or membership to the Church. It reaffirms the longstanding formula of the necessity of the Church for salvation (LG, 14) and goes on to acknowledge that there is some kind of unity in the Spirit by all those who share the same baptism in Christ, even if this unity is not "complete." It moves on to others "who have not yet received the Gospel" and "are related to the People of God in various ways" (LG, 16). This would include not only the Jewish and Islamic people but those of other major world religions, including all those who "seek God with a sincere heart, and, moved by grace, try in their actions to do his will" as their conscience dictates (LG, 16). All of these can and do receive salvation and are united to the people of God in some kind of real, though mysterious, way.

I believe that this ultimately sums up the power of the metaphor "The People of God" for describing the nature and mission of the Church. It admits the primacy of God's power and God's saving plan for all humanity, and the centrality of the Spirit for bringing about the salvation of any person, regardless of their explicit relationship to the Church. This formulation does not diminish the role of the Church in God's plan for salvation but puts it in its proper context—that of the Spirit at work in the world to achieve God's plan in history.

The chapter concludes by emphasizing the sacramental and evangelical role of the visible community of the Church within the wider plan of God for the salvation of the whole world. The Church both prays and works for the realization of the plan God instituted in Jesus Christ, to be carried out in the power of the Holy Spirit, that all of creation should be ultimately united in the divine life. The metaphor of "The People of God" extends the communal dimension of the Mystical Body of Christ beyond that previously articulated at Vatican I or in the encyclical *Mystici Corporis Christi*. Furthermore, it definitively clarifies the doctrine that the Church of Christ extends itself, through the action of the Spirit, well past the boundaries of the visible, structural and hierarchical institution of the Roman Catholic Church. Nevertheless, by doing so, the metaphor also gives a context and a place for these elements within the broader scheme of God's saving plan for the universe, and directly connects these elements to the missions of Christ and the Spirit. This metaphor, therefore, unites the pneumatological, communal and sacramental themes that shape and configure the whole document and the broader ecclesiology it envisions.

Chapter 3: The Church is Hierarchical

No single chapter of this Constitution reflects the theological, ideological, and cultural diversity of the council fathers more than this one on the hierarchical dimension of the Church. This single chapter sustained debate over three sessions of the Council and accounted for the greatest number of revisions and amendments of any single part of the document. Literally hundreds of amendments were offered and thirty-nine successive votes were taken before the full chapter was finally approved.[11] The chapter itself reflects the wide diversity of opinion and the revision and compromise required to reach a consensus on this matter. Consequently, the text itself is not well ordered or fully consistent. The chapter tends to both be repetitive and cover a wide range of issues, sometimes only tenuously related to one another. Some general tendencies emerge, however, and each individual issue discussed can be examined and related to the whole.

The council fathers primarily set out here to complete the work of Vatican I on the nature and function of the hierarchical and institutional dimension of the Body of Christ.[12] They particularly desired to clarify the nature and role of the episcopacy and its relationship to the Roman Pontiff, as well as to balance the nature of papal primacy defined at the previous council. The collegial nature of the episcopacy and its succession to the group of the Twelve chosen by Jesus emerged as the heart of this chapter and the central point of contention among the bishops. Framing the whole hierarchical/institutional structure of the Church within a collegial and, hence, communal context marks one of the most significant developments in ecclesiology offered by the Council.[13]

This chapter thus gives an overall description of the fundamental mission of the hierarchical structure of the Church. It clarifies the nature of the apostles' office and the relationship of their mission to the mission of Christ and his Spirit. Christ stands as the founder and head of the Church; it is to Peter and the apostles, and their successors, that he bequeaths his mission of leading the Church to attain its ultimate goal. The text goes on to clarify the nature of the apostles' office and the relationship of their mission to the mission of the Spirit. Christ called the apostles and "constituted" them in the "form of a college or permanent assembly, at the head of which he placed Peter, chosen from amongst them" (LG, 19). Their communal character extends the preaching ministry of Jesus himself through its organizational life. For this reason, "they were fully confirmed in this mission on the day of Pentecost" when the Holy Spirit descended upon them (LG, 19). Their mission, inaugurated by Jesus during his lifetime, became fully realized only when it was directly united with the mission of Christ's Spirit and came under the Spirit's guidance and ongoing influence. Episcopal consecration literally makes each bishop a "representative" of Christ but also contextualizes this personal charism within the college of other bishops, under the leadership of the Roman Pontiff. Episcopal consecration simultaneously relates the bishop directly to Jesus Christ and to the universal episcopal college. In this sense, one's individual consecration, though the highest form of ministerial office, always functions within and is qualified by the hierarchical communion of other bishops.

An ecumenical council represents the greatest sign of the nature of the episcopacy. In this context, the worldwide college of bishops in union with their head, the pope, settles "conjointly, in a decision rendered balanced and equitable by the advice of many, all questions of major importance" (LG, 22). The text immediately qualifies this statement by reinforcing the point that no council has any authority whatsoever unless united with the Roman Pontiff. Similarly the bishop of Rome, as the "vicar of Christ," has "full, supreme and universal authority over the whole Church, a power which he can always exercise unhindered" (LG, 22). While the text seemingly equivocates as to the source of highest authority in the Church—the pope himself and a universal council of bishops united with its head—it ultimately points to the ecumenical council as the fullest expression of the universal and collegial character of the hierarchy and its hegemony over the Church. It is the council, without prejudice to the genuine and autonomous power of the papacy, that manifests the organic structure and communal harmony of the Church empowered by the Holy Spirit (LG, 22).

Paragraph 23 directs its attention to outlining the relationship of each bishop, and hence each diocese, to the universal Church. The text proposes the following formula:

> The Roman Pontiff, as the successor of Peter, is the perpetual and visible source and foundation of unity both of the bishops and of the whole company of the faithful. The individual bishops are the visible source and foundation of unity in their own particular Churches, which are constituted after the model of the universal Church; it is in these and formed out of them that the one and unique Catholic Church exists. (LG, 23)

This formula suggests a certain primacy of the universal Church over the individual Churches in that the former acts as the model of the latter, and the function of the individual bishop reflects the function of the pope. Nevertheless, the universal Church does not exist, nor can it be described, apart from its composition of the individual Churches. The universal Church exists in each individual Church, and the universal Church is "formed out of" these individual Churches. This leads to the conclusion that the "whole Mystical Body" can be described as a "corporate body of Churches" (LG, 23). The universal Church exists, therefore, precisely as a communion of individual ecclesial communities in such a way that there remains a mutual interrelationship and interdependence between the universal and the particular church.

This balance between the universal and the particular receives further articulation later in the same paragraph:

> It has come about through divine providence that, in the course of time, different Churches set up in various places by the apostles and their successors joined together in a multiplicity of organically united groups which, whilst safeguarding the unity of the faith and

the unique divine structure of the universal Church, have their own discipline, enjoy their own liturgical usage and inherit a theological and spiritual patrimony. . . . This multiplicity of local Churches, unified in a common effort, shows all the more resplendently the catholicity of the undivided Church. (LG, 23)

By envisioning the Church as an organically connected living body, incorporating many diverse parts into a single common life, the text offers an understanding of the Church that truly balances the universal and the individual, the worldwide and local, the whole and the particular, without subjugating one to the other. This balanced and genuinely catholic definition of the Church reveals again, I believe, the theological vision grounding all of *Lumen Gentium*, and it offers a hopeful and renewed understanding of the hierarchical dimension of the Church.

The text then goes on to examine the office of the local bishop—his authority, duties, responsibilities and relationship to the members of his diocese. Within this context, the nature of infallibility, especially as it applies to the Roman Pontiff, emerges for further clarification. The office of bishop functions within the ecclesial community primarily and "strictly" as a "service" (*diakonia*) to the Church (LG, 24). This service includes many duties and responsibilities, among which "preaching the Gospel has the pride of place" (LG, 25). To enable the efficacy of this preaching, bishops are endowed "with the authority of Christ" (LG, 25). This authority validates the teaching role the bishops derive from their mandate to preach the gospel. As the authentic and primary teachers in the community of believers, the bishops act with the fullest authority in their individual communities, and in "communion" with the college of bishops and with the pope they hold the supreme teaching authority in the Church (LG, 25). Given both their mandate and their authority, the text states that "the faithful, for their part, are obliged to submit to their bishops' decisions, made in the name of Christ, in matters of faith and morals, and to adhere to it with a ready allegiance of mind" (LG, 25).

The submission of the faithful to the decision of their bishops extends in a special way to the Roman Pontiff. His teaching authority requires the highest degree of submission of intellect and will even when he is not speaking "infallibly" per se. The infallibility of the pope, first articulated at Vatican I, is reaffirmed here, and even clarified to some extent. Infallibility exists first of all with the whole Church by virtue of the will of God. Papal infallibility derives from this broader ecclesial infallibility:

> The Roman Pontiff, head of the college of bishops, enjoys this infallibility in virtue of his office, when, as supreme pastor and teacher . . . he proclaims in an absolute decision a doctrine pertaining to faith or morals. For that reason his definitions are said to be irreformable by their very nature and not by reason of the assent of the Church . . . and do not admit of appeal to any other tribunal. (LG, 25)

In the Roman Pontiff, therefore, "the Church's charism of infallibility is present in a singular way" (LG, 25).[14]

The bishops individually do not possess this charism of infallibility. Nevertheless, when they act, in various ways (outlined in the text) in communion with the whole college of bishops under the headship of the Roman Pontiff, they can be said to be acting infallibly. A universal and ecumenical council of the whole college of bishops exhibits this capacity most clearly. This part of the text concludes by clarifying that even when the pope, or the bishops in union with the pope, choose to speak infallibly they do so in conformity with divine revelation, not by way of adding to it. The bishops can clarify, give new expression, or apply in contemporary terms the divine "deposit of faith" (LG, 25). The Constitution insists, however, that "they do not . . . admit any new public revelation as pertaining to the divine deposit of faith" (LG, 25).

Paragraph 26 emphasizes the fullness of the local Church as presided over by the bishop (literally in the case of the eucharistic liturgy). The text states:

> This Church of Christ is really present in all legitimately organized local groups of the faithful, which, insofar as they are united to their pastors, are also quite appropriately called churches in the New Testament. . . . In each altar community, under the sacred ministry of the bishop, a manifest symbol is to be seen of that charity and "unity of the mystical body, without which there can be no salvation." (LG, 26)

This implies that each local Church itself is composed of a communion of smaller communities, somewhat on the analogy of the universal Church. These smaller communities genuinely represent and participate in the Church of Christ. The text likewise suggests that the primary characteristic of these communities is their participation in the eucharist at some level ("altar communities"), and that, however small and diverse, they are in a relationship with and "under" the guidance of the local bishop.

The sacred power is entrusted by Christ to each individual bishop. While affirming the collegial character of the episcopacy and the hegemony of the Roman Pontiff, the document clarifies the autonomy of each bishop, who exercises his authority "personally in the name of Christ." This authority is "proper, ordinary and immediate," although it is always subject to the "supreme authority of the Church" under certain circumstances (LG, 27). Nevertheless, the permanent and daily responsibilities of their office are "entrusted to them fully; nor are they to be regarded as vicars of the Roman Pontiff" (LG, 27). The text strongly asserts that each bishop exercises in his own right the power he is given by consecration and office, and he is to genuinely be considered, under the influence of the Holy Spirit, head of his individual Church. The bishop and the faithful of his Church should be united and related in such a way that "all things may conspire toward harmonious unity" (LG, 27). This indicates that a full and autonomous nature characterizes both the bishop and the church over which he presides. This strong assertion in the document tends to balance universal and absolute papal hegemony often assumed by Catholic ecclesiology after Vatican I.

The priests, together with their bishop, form a "unique sacerdotal college (*presbyterium*)" (LG, 28). This presbyterial college acts in cooperation with the episcopal college to serve the people of God. The priests, for their part, function as the "support and mouthpiece" of the episcopal college at local levels (LG, 28). And while members of the presbyterial college do not share full pontifical power, they have their own "proper power" conferred on them through the sacrament of orders wherein they act, especially in the liturgical and sacramental sphere, in the person of Christ (LG, 28). It is their special duty to preside over the local communities that constitute an individual Church under the local bishop. In this sense, priests have a significant and direct effect on the literal building up of the Body of Christ and the unity of the whole people of God.

"At the lower level of the hierarchy are to be found deacons, who receive the imposition of hands 'not unto the priesthood, but unto the ministry'" (LG, 29). This rather awkward statement seems to imply that diaconate ordination marks a call to ministry in a general sense. The deacons also form a brotherhood or college that cooperates in a similar, though distinct, way as the presbyterial college, to aid and assist the bishop and episcopal college in their duties. This council moved to restore the diaconate as a proper and permanent rank in the hierarchy, even opening up the possibility that married men could receive this order. While sharing in some liturgical responsibilities, especially in cooperation with priests and in those situations where priests are absent, the primary task of the deacon envisioned by the Council would be the works of charity and the "functions of administration" (LG, 29).

Chapter 4: The Laity

Chapter 4 can be interpreted in various ways. In one sense it functions as the obvious complement to chapter 3: having discussed the hierarchy in some detail, the document now turns its attention to the rest of the Church. This can be read as a somewhat patronizing attempt to include the great majority of the membership derivatively in the life of the Church by placing them in the shadow of the hierarchy. Following the lead of Congar as outlined earlier, however, I believe that this chapter acts as the "twin foci" of the discussion on the nature and mission of the visible and institutional Church prompted by chapter 2's wider discussion of the people of God. In this sense, chapter 4 completes chapter 3 by presuming that the laity share, in a different but equally important way, in the Catholic Church and its place in the wider people of God. In the context of the first two chapters of the constitution, the laity clearly do not act as adjuncts to the hierarchy. Rather, the divine institution and indispensability of the laity for the life of the Church is as given and indisputable as that of the hierarchy.

The text defines the laity in the following way:

> The term "laity" is here understood to mean all the faithful except those in Holy Orders and those who belong to the religious state approved by the Church. That is, the faithful who by Baptism are incorporated into Christ, are placed in the People of God, and in their own way share the priestly, prophetic and kingly office of Christ, and to the best of their ability carry on the mission of the whole Christian people in the Church and in the world. (LG, 31)

This definition places the emphasis on Initiation as the act of incorporation, and extends the mission of the whole Christian people to the lay members of the Catholic Church in a special way. This mission directs the laity both to the Church and to the world. It suggests that they are not to be considered merely passive agents of the hierarchy but have their own distinct and significant contribution to make.

The laity have a "special vocation" to build up the kingdom of God within the "temporal" world (LG, 31). Led by the Spirit they are called by God to "the sanctification of the world, as from within like leaven" (LG, 31). The laity "enjoy the principal role" in the Church's universal mission to bring about the reign of justice, peace, and love (LG, 36). They are appointed by the Lord himself to "impregnate culture and human works with moral value" (LG, 36). Their share in the priestly, prophetic and kingly office of Jesus Christ expresses itself most fully in their actions outside the explicit institutional boundaries of the Church.

Within the Church itself, the laity possess by divine right "a true equality . . . with regard to the dignity and to the activity which is common to all the faithful in the building up of the Body of Christ" (LG, 32). Clearly, the bishops desired to balance the relationship between the laity and those in holy orders. While maintaining the existing hierarchical hegemony in regard to the internal governing of the Church, the Council was able to articulate a more active and essential role for the laity in the life and mission of the Church. If the emphasis in chapter 3 was on the role of the hierarchy in building up the internal unity and publicly articulating the message and faith of the Church, then the emphasis in chapter 4 shifts to the role the laity play in actually effecting the mission of the Church as an instrument of the reign of God in concrete historical circumstances. In the light of the whole dogmatic and pastoral Constitutions, the role of the laity does not emerge as underestimated or insignificant.

Chapter 5: The Call to Holiness

I believe that this chapter functions primarily as both a conclusion and a unifying link between chapters 3, 4 and 6 (Religious Life). While these three chapters outline the distinctions and diversity within the community of faith, chapter 5 expresses what all the faithful, through baptism, share in common as members of the Church. Through the sacrament of Initiation the faithful are not only incorporated into the visible Church, but they are endowed with a genuine share in her enlivening spirit. The gift of the Holy Spirit and the subsequent vocation to live as Jesus lived—the life of perfection or holiness—is given to every member of the Church regardless of what state or condition he or she occupies within the actual living community. As the text states:

> Therefore all in the Church, whether they belong to the hierarchy or are cared for by it, are called to holiness. . . This holiness of the Church is constantly shown forth in the fruits of grace which the Spirit produces in the faithful and so it must be; it is expressed in many ways by the individuals, each in his own state of life, tend to the perfection of love, thus helping others to grow in holiness. (LG, 39)

The reciprocal nature of this call to holiness implies an interconnectedness within the body whereby each believer influences and strengthens other members in a way that requires a genuine sharing of life to achieve holiness. This mutual effect in the growth of holiness manifests the interior working of the Holy Spirit in the life of each individual and the community as a whole. In this sense, chapter 5 marks the richest expression of the actual working of the Holy Spirit in the life of the community discussed thus far in the documents. The primary role of the Spirit lies precisely in prompting and coordinating the unifying action of love within the community, which in turn elicits and enables further acts of love that enhance the corporate unity still more. The Holy Spirit, therefore, acts as the bond of love within the community, uniting each individual's specific vocation into a common one, whereby the community as a whole receives a call to holiness: "The forms and tasks of life are many but holiness is one"

(LG, 41). The sanctifying action of the Holy Spirit leads the whole Church, regardless of any internal differentiation of gifts, along the single path of holiness marked out for the Church by the life and mission of Jesus Christ. The fundamental distinction between the ordained and lay—the hierarchy and the rest of the baptized—is relativized by the transcendent call to holiness and the specific demands of charity.

Chapter 6: Religious

Religious life flourished in the period of time between the Vatican Councils in a way that was unprecedented since the Baroque period. I believe that much of the impetus for this growth and diversification of religious life stemmed from the ecclesiology of the *societas perfecta* described earlier. Within the context of this ecclesiology, religious life occupied a clearly defined and necessary place. The religious who ran the schools, hospitals, and other social and cultural institutions of the Church's distinct social life were indispensable to the life of the community. The supplanting of the ecclesiology of the *societas perfecta* obviously imperiled the clarity of role and distinction of place religious life enjoyed within the Body of Christ. Chapter 6 attempts to discuss religious life, undeniably essential to the life of the Church, within the context of the new ecclesiology emerging at Vatican II.

The distinctiveness of religious life lies in the special charism ("gift of grace") it possesses and shares with the rest of the community. This charism generally implies that the religious will lead a unique style of life, but not one separate from or greater than the call of all Christians to holiness. Religious life, therefore, simply expresses one way of being a Christian. Religious communities function within and serve the Church as a community of communities, which in turn serve the wider human community. Religious communities exist within the wider Church in a sacramental way analogous to how the Church exists for the wider world: as a sign and instrument of the reign of God.

Chapter 7: The Pilgrim Church

This chapter serves as a conclusion to the document by dwelling particularly on the eschatological dimension of the Church's life and mission. The term "pilgrim" refers back to the first two chapters, while also directing the attention of the reader beyond the examination of the Church's internal nature and purpose that has characterized the preceding four chapters. It analyzes the goal or ends of the Church's mission as well as its transitory and incomplete incarnation in any concrete and historical situation. Furthermore, it attempts to articulate the profound connection (communion) between the historically and universally present Church of Christ with the eternal community of saints already gathered in the heavenly kingdom. In other words, this chapter completes the examination of the structures and function of the temporal, institutional Church, by explaining its eternal and supernatural dimension.

While the ultimate end of the Church and world may be the same, their present conditions and functions remain quite different. The Church, as the Body of Christ, acknowledges, anticipates and prefigures the coming salvation. The community of believers, therefore, acts as pilgrims who journey along with the world, but with the hope for and assurance of a clear destination. They are not alone on this journey. The pilgrims are not only united with all those throughout the world who walk this same path in the same Spirit, but they are profoundly united with all those who have gone before them in faith and have already arrived at their shared destiny. The term "communion of saints" traditionally denotes this rich community of pilgrims that transcends the limits of both time and space.

Chapter 8: Our Lady

Originally this chapter existed as a separate schema from the one on the nature of the Church. For a variety of reasons the theological commission of the Council decided to incorporate it into the dogmatic Constitution of the Church.[15] The primary emphasis of the text asserts the "pre-eminent" and "wholly unique" membership of Mary in the Mystical Body of Christ in that she acts as the fundamental model of Christian discipleship (LG, 53). While strongly insisting on the sole mediatorship of Christ in the salvation of humanity and the distinctive mission of the Spirit in continuing and empowering Christ's work of our redemption, this chapter serves to honor Mary precisely in her role as a human person responding to God's initiative of grace and redemption in Christ. The document, by its own admission (LG, 54), does not seek to offer a full explanation of the doctrine of Mary, but rather to pass on in a new synthesis the long-standing tradition regarding Mary's special role in the Incarnation and the Church.

At the heart of this analysis of Mary's role lies the assertion that Mary was not simply a passive and accidental participant of God's gracious activity. Rather, Mary freely chose to cooperate with God's plans in a way that genuinely advanced the work of human redemption.[16] This insistence on Mary's active cooperation with grace and authentic agency in God's plan is consistent with the entire theology of grace underlying the document. This understanding of grace, which appreciates the necessity of human cooperation and agency, enables the Council to explain the evangelical and sacramental character of the Church as a whole. The whole community of believers thus acts not merely as some kind of passive association of like-minded persons but as a community of persons who have received and accepted the call to act as signs and instruments of God's saving plan for all creation. In this context, the document's presentation of Mary as a type or model of the discipleship that characterizes all Christians seems appropriate. The chapter succeeds in balancing cautions against exaggerating the role of Mary with affirmations of the special place she holds as a direct participant in the Incarnation and as the

principal model of the virtues necessary to build up both the
Church and the Kingdom.

IV. Summaries of Some Decrees and Declarations Bridging *Lumen Gentium* and *Gaudium et Spes*

Unitatis Redintegratio, Christus Dominus, Nostra Aetate,
and *Apostolicam Actuositatem*

Unitatis Redintegratio[17] emerged as one of the most significant documents produced during the third session of the
Council. It developed in tandem with *Lumen Gentium* and
reflects a continuity and elaboration of the basic principles
laid out in that document. Nevertheless, this decree offers
some important clarifications and even extends the ecumenical content of the Constitution. In what follows I shall offer a
brief summary of a few of its more significant statements.

The decree begins by asserting that the "restoration of unity
among all Christians is one of the principal concerns of the
Second Vatican Council" (UR, 1). The Council identifies the
disunity among Christians as a source of grave scandal to both
Christians and non-Christians, and a severe obstacle to the
credible preaching of the gospel by any Christian community.

The Council here reiterates early admissions that all sides
are to blame for the current state of division. The text also reaffirms that all of the baptized, and their respective commu-
nions, are put into "some, though imperfect, communion with
the Catholic Church" (UR, 3). The text also reasserts that
many of these Christian communities outside the visible Catholic community contain and foster the "most significant
elements and endowments" of the one Church of Christ (UR,
2). Thus, all these communities together can be considered as
constituting the one Church of Christ, even though only the
Roman Catholic Church still retains the full unity of faith originally bestowed by Jesus Christ. This unity "subsists" in the
Catholic Church itself, and exists as something she can share

with all other communities (UR, 2).[18] This situation calls for a sincere and heartfelt dialogue and growing charitable communion between all the separated communities.

Christus Dominus basically reiterates and elaborates on chapter 3 of *Lumen Gentium*, "The Church is Hierarchical." The central focus of this document emerges as a reassertion and clarification of the collegial nature of episcopal consecration and, hence, the relationship of the universal Church to each particular church (CD, 1–3).

Nostra Aetate states that "All men form but one community" (NA, 1). This document specifies and extends the far-reaching principle in both *Lumen Gentium* and *Gaudium et Spes* that God as creator of all humanity also serves as the fundamental source of unity underlying all creation. It also emphasizes the universal saving will of God extended to all humanity through Christ and the radical presence of God's Spirit genuinely working in all human hearts and communities. Without denying the unique function of Jesus Christ, and the Church's deposit of revelation, "the Catholic Church rejects nothing of what is true and holy" in other world religions (NA, 2).

Apostolicam Actuositatem similarly reiterates and expands on most of the principles outlined in *Lumen Gentium* that eventually would be set out in *Gaudium et Spes*. The specific emphasis here is on the active apostolate of the laity. The text clarifies the central role that the laity play in the Church's mission to the world, and examines the many various spiritualities and vocations that form the laity's general vocation. This statement, and similar ones throughout the document, actually advance the vision of *Lumen Gentium* (especially chapters 1 and 2) by giving the laity their own proper rights and duties both within the Church and in the Church's broader mission to the world.[19] This enhanced view of the apostolate of all Christians will influence the whole direction of *Gaudium et Spes*. The existence of this universal vocation and the general manifestation of the charisms it implies tend to blur the dualistic distinction between the "hierarchical principle" and the "communal principle" characteristic of most ecclesiology before the Council, even that focused on the role of the laity (e.g., Congar). Finally, the document emphasizes the need for solid training and education for all lay people so that they may more fully understand and accomplish their vocation (AA, 28–32).

Dignitatis Humanae[20]

Although finally approved only the day before the close of the Council (December 7, 1965), the discussion on this document occurred at three sessions of the Council and resulted from much work done between the last three sessions.[21] The document stands as one of the most controversial texts debated during the Council, although it won overwhelming approval in the end. The subtitle of the document best expresses its content: "On the Right of the Person and Communities to Social and Civil Liberty in Religious Matters." Rooted in the inherent dignity of the human person, the document offers an extensive treatment on the fundamental freedom of conscience and activity owed to each person by both the Church and state.

The heart of this document lies, I believe, in the opening paragraph of the first chapter:

> The Vatican Council declares that the human person has the right to religious freedom. Freedom of this kind means that all men should be immune from coercion on the part of individuals, social groups and every human power so that, within due limits, nobody is forced to act against his convictions nor is anyone constrained from acting in accordance with his convictions in religious matters in private or public, alone or in association with others . . . the right to religious freedom is based on the very dignity of the human person as known through the revealed word of God and by reason itself. (DH, 2)

This fundamental freedom from any sort of coercion means that truth, understanding, and knowledge can never be imposed on human beings. Each person still has a natural and moral obligation to seek the truth, and to use all available means to obtain genuine knowledge of the world and the meaning and purpose of human life. The ultimate responsibility for this search, however, lies in the very nature of the individual person and not in any external agent of civil or religious authority. For this reason, the immunity from coercion "continues to exist even in those who do not live up to their obligation of seeking truth and adhering to it" (DH, 2). As long as the "just requirements of public order" remain intact, humans possess a fundamental right to live even in ignorance, error, or misunderstanding. The text goes on to discuss truth and how it relates to individuals and communities.

The authors of the document want to insist that this declaration does not represent totally new teaching, although it obviously emerges as a new and clearer articulation of the sources of revelation and the long tradition of teaching and doctrine regarding human conscience and the divine law (DH, 9–15). The text discovers in scripture itself the profound appreciation for the infinite dignity of the human person. Furthermore, the earliest actions of both Christ and his apostles remind us that the kind of truth known by faith comes to us as a gift and invitation. Neither God nor those legitimately acting in the name of God resort to coercion or force in the service and offer of truth. The nature of faith itself evokes the profound mystery of human liberty and God's choice to create humans with both rational minds and the freedom to use these minds in various and even contradictory ways. In this sense, the Council proclaims that religious liberty exists in its own right not just as a necessary element of the common good but as the very will of God for human beings and human society. God creates humans to know and love God but with the freedom finally to accept or reject this divine offer, each one in his or her own unique way. The mystery of the divine plan demands that both Church and state respect this divine choice and act always in accord with ultimate dignity of the human person (DH, 13).

V. Gaudium et Spes

This document, the *Pastoral Constitution on the Church in the Modern World*, marks not only the longest single text promulgated by the Council but can also be described as unique in the history of conciliar documents. The term "pastoral" best evokes its nature. Through this document the bishops attempted to directly communicate their understanding of the Church and its relationship with the wider world to people of different faiths, cultures, and world views. While resting on and further articulating the solid doctrinal principles set forth in *Lumen Gentium* and the intervening declarations and decrees from all four sessions, this document seeks to apply these principles to the concrete situation of the modern world and explain the implications to common people. The council fathers, therefore, hoped both to engage an audience not usually considered when making doctrinal decisions and to interpret these decisions' concrete and historical implications. The term "pastoral" also reflects the emphasis in the document on the special ministry and role of the laity in the mission of the Church. For these reasons, I believe, this "pastoral" Constitution offers both a summary and self-interpretation of the more than three years of Council deliberations on a wide variety of issues and topics.

The document is divided into two parts. The first develops and explains the Church's understanding of the human person, the relationship between the human person and society/culture, and the Church's relationship to this nexus of human beings in cultures and societies that in turn comprise the "world." The second part seeks to interpret and apply the principles developed in the first, in terms of five particularly urgent and critical areas or problems faced by the modern world. I will concentrate on the first part and only briefly summarize the issues and conclusions treated at great length in the second.

Title and Preface

The title chosen for this document evokes comment not only because of the inclusion of the term "pastoral" but also because of the term "in." In the light of earlier discussions, examining the Church "in" the modern world appears quite significant. By choosing to consider the Church in the world, the Council effectively set aside the ecclesiology of the *societas perfecta*, which specifically asserted the juxtaposition of Church and world. Likewise, this particular phrasing also challenges those ecclesiologies of the Mystical Body of Christ that held an implicit dualism between Church and world. From the outset, this Council places the Church in the context of the wider human community and creation as a whole. The Church, therefore, does not exist above, alongside, or separately from the world. While the full meaning of the term "world" itself will require a more thorough elaboration, the title truly determines the fundamental orientation of the whole document.

The first paragraph of the preface stands as one of the most poetic and profound statements to emerge from the Council. Central to this statement is the genuine and intense solidarity Christians share with the rest of humanity: "Nothing that is truly human fails to find an echo in their hearts" (GS, 1). Christianity does not exist as some separate state of existence but as a particular way of being human.

The document employs fundamental theological categories to define Christianity: community, the Holy Spirit, and sacrament. Christians live as a community within the wider human community. Christ's Spirit guides and animates this community in a special way. The unique presence of the Spirit enables the Christian community to act as a sign and instrument of God's plan for the rest of humanity. Nevertheless, both the Christian and the human communities share the same destiny.

Because of the deep interconnection between the Christian and the wider human communities, the Council wanted to address its message to the whole world. Paragraph 2 defines the world as "the whole human family seen in the context of everything which envelops it" (GS, 2). Because the Church and the world share the same source and destiny, their relationship requires that they not only live together but enter into a genuine "dialogue" that seriously addresses the problems and issues, hopes and fears that all human beings face (GS, 3). The Church, therefore, must offer to share her many resources with the wider community while at the same time opening her own life to cooperate with the world in building up the reign of God that awaits all creation. The Church's and humanity's destinies are irrevocably linked. This realization offers the only true starting point from which any analysis of the relationship between the Church and the world can be fully explored.

Introduction: The Situation of Man in the World Today

The document goes on to address current situations, stressing the Church's responsibility to initiate dialogue with the world. The world finds itself caught in the midst of incredible growth, opportunity, and interdependence, at the same time that these very realities unsettle the stability of previous eras and enable the development of new and more deadly (both spiritually and physically) forms of human creativity. The Council realizes that this situation is rooted in growing human "self-awareness" and a "broadening mastery over time" (GS, 5). This emerging world view carries with it possibilities both incredible and frightening. The Church cannot ignore either the threat or challenge of this new moment in history. This worldwide awareness of both the hope and fear of the current situation offers a profound opportunity to the Church. Through the person and message of Jesus Christ, she knows the answers to some of the most urgent questions facing human beings today.

Part I: The Church and Man's Vocation

The first part of this document essentially divides into four interrelated chapters, presenting a theological interpretation of the human person, the world, and the Church's mission in the light of these. The principles enunciated may be described in general as anthropological (chapter 1), sociological (chapter 2), cosmological (chapter 3), and ecclesiological (chapter 4). These four chapters build on one another and all are interpreted in the light of Christian theology and contemporary cultural dynamics, forming a comprehensive theological synthesis.

Chapter 1: The Dignity of the Human Person

That human beings were created in "the image of God" acts as the primary insight, drawn from scripture, for probing the mystery of the human person. This insight responds to one of the most fundamental questions troubling humankind in the modern world: What is a human being? The often conflicting and contradictory answers to this question lie at the heart of the modern dilemma. From revelation, we know that God did not create human beings to remain solitary beings. Human persons exist always as persons in "communion":

> For by his innermost nature man is a social being; and
> if he does not enter into relations with others he can
> neither live nor develop his gifts. (GS, 12)

This social nature of the individual person presumes that men and women are most fully human when they enter into collaborative and mutually shared lives and activities. It goes on to discuss sin, grace, freedom, atheism, and finally how the Incarnation clarifies the nature of human dignity. Because human nature was "assumed, not absorbed" by Jesus Christ, each human person is united to Christ in a special way (GS, 22). Human beings are "conformed to the image of the Son" through the Incarnation and therefore receive his Spirit as the fruit of this conformity (GS, 22). The presence of Christ's Spirit in every human person implies that God excludes no one *a priori* from the gift of grace. Human dignity resides ultimately in the fact that all people have access to the divine life through the presence of God's Spirit in each person's life. As the text states in conclusion:

> All this holds true not for Christians only but also for all men of good will in whose hearts grace is active invisibly. For since Christ died for all, and since all men are in fact called to the same destiny, which is divine, we must hold that the Holy Spirit offers *to all* the possibility of being made partners, in a way known to God, in the paschal mystery. (GS, 22) (italics mine)

Chapter 2: The Community of Mankind

This chapter asserts that the "intense development of interpersonal relationships" in the world today represents a significant "sign of the times" (GS, 23)—in a way it represents God's plan. Scripture reveals that God designed the human person to be naturally "communitarian" (GS, 23). Christian sociology is grounded in the assumption that God created and calls all human beings to live together as one family united by a spirit of filial charity (GS, 24). The human vocation to community denotes more than just a natural tendency toward socialization; it represents, rather, humanity's participation in the divine life itself. The text states that there exists a "certain parallel" between the divine triune life and the social/communal life of human persons (GS, 24). From a Christian viewpoint the full humanity of each person can only be realized in community.

This communitarian or social dimension to the individual manifests itself most appropriately in the dedication of each person to provide for the well-being of society as a whole. There exists a genuine interdependence between the individual person and the wider society such that the welfare of one affects all and vice-versa. This social nature of the human person implies that "society is not something accessory to man himself" (GS, 25). Everyone develops a unique identity and configuration of talents, gifts, and traits precisely through his or her interaction and dialogue with the wider community of which each person is an integral part. Some levels of community come by nature to the individual, like family and the political and cultural community in which one is immersed from birth. Other types of social groupings and communities emerge from the free choice of the person. Regardless of their origin, however, no individual can ever be free from the influence of and dependence on multiple forms of community and social life.

The text goes on to speak about the common good, the work of the Holy Spirit in organizing and coordinating mutually dependent communities, and respect for every human person. This insistence on the communal character of the individual person and of morality rests finally on a vision of human destiny wherein each person will be saved not just as an individual but as a member of a community (GS, 32). The fullness of human life comes from living in a social unity that derives from Jesus Christ and from acting as one "people" in service to God and God's creation. In other words, this chapter maintains that human sanctity cannot be separated from the sanctification of the wider communal and social structures in which the individual participates. There exists then a certain "solidarity" between all the peoples of the earth in their common source and destiny, so much so that God wills that all be saved as much as that one be saved (GS, 32). God's Spirit directs and guides this process of gradually building up the communion of all persons with one another and with God until "that day when it will be brought to fulfillment; on that day mankind, saved by grace, will offer perfect glory to God as the family beloved by God and of Christ their brother" (GS, 32). In short, the Christian anthropology articulated by this document finds its reflection, source, and goal in the divine life of the Trinity itself.

Chapter 3: Man's Activity in the Universe

The document moves on to discern the place of human activity within the wider context of the dynamic cosmic process. Central to this context is the observation that "the human family is gradually coming to recognize itself and constitute itself as one single community over the whole earth" (GS, 33). This implies that the growth and development of human culture cannot be separated from the "mysterious design" of God for the universe (GS, 34). This overall vision of human activity suggests the following "norm" for regulating human activity:

> to harmonize with the authentic interests of the human race, in accordance with God's will and design, and to enable men as individuals and as members of society to pursue and fulfill their total vocation. (GS, 35)

All of this means that no aspect of human activity or life can be considered beyond the pale of God's own plans for and activity within the universe. It thus lays to rest any dualism or dichotomy that may have characterized earlier interpretations of the relationship between God and the world. The world does have a certain autonomy, and human activity can thus advance or obstruct God's activity. God, however, never abandons the world but works to redeem it. This profound and mysterious interaction between God and the universe, mediated through human conscious activity, represents the fullest expression of the Church's understanding of both grace and creation.

Chapter 4: Role of the Church in the Modern World

Dialogue, mutuality, and reciprocity serve as the primary leitmotifs running through this last chapter of Part 1. Drawing on the ecclesiology of *Lumen Gentium*, it begins by reaffirming that the Church exists as both a visibly organized and institutionalized society and as a "spiritual community" (GS, 40).[22]

Critical to this definition remains the assumption that the Church is constituted by Christ in time and animated by the Holy Spirit through history. The Church, therefore, "travels the same journey as all mankind and shares the same earthly lot with the world" (GS, 40). The Church and the world "penetrate" one another, with the Church acting as salt, leaven, and light within the world, converting and renewing it in union with the work of the Spirit. The Church's mission becomes particularly clear in this light:

> In pursuing its own salvific purpose not only does the Church communicate divine life to men but in a certain sense it casts the reflected light of that divine life over all the earth, notably in the way it heals and elevates the dignity of the human person, in the way it consolidates society, and endows the daily activity of men with a deeper sense of meaning. The Church, then, believes it can contribute much to humanizing the family of man and its history through each of its members and the community as a whole. (GS, 40)

This ongoing process of "humanization" reflects the Church's belief that from the beginning God's grace acts within human history and the universe and exists outside the explicit and visible boundaries of the Church. Furthermore, the Catholic Church acknowledges and values "what other Christian Churches and ecclesial communities have contributed and are contributing cooperatively to the realization of this aim" (GS, 40). The Church, in all her manifestations, works together in "mutual exchange" with all the positive and life-giving movements and communities in the world to prepare the universe, both consciously and unconsciously, for the coming reign of God. While the Church has something profoundly important to offer the world, the world cooperates with the Church in its mission and actually expands it by contributing its unique gifts and activities (GS, 40).

Chapter 4 then proceeds to enumerate the Church's contribution to individuals, society, and "human activity" and the world's contribution to the Church. The laity emerge in this document as fully active participants in the life of the Church. They are no longer consigned to passive obedience to clerical initiatives but can themselves inaugurate and promote the building up of the reign of God in all dimensions of their lives. In this way the Church offers the world a wealth of resources, both individual and communal, and, empowered by the Holy Spirit, provides the rest of society with the vision and dynamism it needs to improve human society and achieve its destiny. And as a visible social structure, the Church can be enriched by the "evolution of social life" in general (GS, 44). Whatever contributes to the development and enhancement of community in general can assist the Church in its ongoing desire to be more fully a community of believers.

Part II: Some More Urgent Problems

Space permits only a fleeting glance at the second part of this document. It applies the principles enunciated in the first in terms of five critical areas of the "modern world" that the Council determined needed to be addressed. These five areas are entitled as follows: "The Dignity of Marriage and the Family"; "Proper Development of Culture"; "Economic and Social Life"; "The Political Community"; and "Fostering of Peace and Establishment of a Community of Nations." In each of these chapters the issues and problems are articulated and analyzed, Church teaching and the tradition regarding these issues are introduced and placed in dialogue with the situation, and some practical considerations and ecclesiological implications emerge.

Guiding both the analysis and the theological reflection of each of these chapters remain the central themes that characterize the first part of the document: the fundamental dignity of the human person; the communal and social nature of individual and personal development; the priority of the common good in determining right conduct and ethical action; the need for the Church to act both as an example and a means of promoting and building unity between persons and communities and nations; the precedence and necessity of justice and humanization at basic social and cultural levels as the foundation for explicit evangelization; the need for ongoing and mutual dialogue between the Church (both lay and clerical) and the many diverse and divergent streams of modern societies and cultures.

Conclusion

This document concludes with both a call and paean to the integrity and unity of the people of God. The text returns to the fundamental characteristics that served as the subject of the document's first part. Central to this remains an unequivocal call to the Church for a renewal and intensification of her mission to act as a sacrament of the original plan and coming reign of God in the world. This sacramental mission calls the Church to conversion and requires that it make a deeper commitment to achieve the unity of the children of God which it proclaims. As the text states:

> Such a mission requires us first of all to create in the Church itself mutual esteem, reverence and harmony, and acknowledge all legitimate diversity; in this way all who constitute the one people of God will be able to engage in ever more fruitful dialogue, whether they are pastors or other members of the faithful. For the ties which unite the faithful together are stronger than those which separate them: let there be unity in what is necessary, freedom in what is doubtful, and charity in everything. (GS, 92)

The Church acts in the world as the "harbinger" of unity and peace and the visible instrument of the Holy Spirit's work to achieve the plan of God for the whole universe. For this reason the text concludes with a clarion call to a dialogue between the Church and the world that "excludes nobody," including those who hate and persecute her.

VI. Three Heuristic Keys to the Documents: Three Interrelated Concepts

Gaudium et Spes clarifies and fulfills the promise of *Lumen Gentium*. I detect a strong correlation between the fundamental principles of ecclesiology outlined in *Lumen Gentium* and the elaboration and application of those principles in *Gaudium et Spes*. I would argue for the continuity of the documents and define *Gaudium et Spes* as the legitimate and proper interpretation of the doctrine articulated in *Lumen Gentium*. The effect of this profound relationship means that any general interpretation of ecclesiology in the light of Vatican II must fully incorporate both Constitutions on the nature of the Church. From both of these, in line with other constitutions and decrees of the Council, I believe it is possible to draw fairly coherent norms and a cohesive overall schema on the nature and mission of the Church.

This schema appears succinctly in the passage in *Gaudium et Spes* where the council fathers offer a definition of Christian life:

> For theirs is a *community* composed of men, of men who, guided by the *Holy Spirit*, press onwards towards the kingdom of the Father and are *bearers of a message of salvation* intended for all men. (GS, 1) (italics mine)

Throughout the documents one detects a consistent interweaving of these three interrelated concepts to define, clarify, and explain the nature and mission of the Church. Besides what I would term a total displacement of the official pre-conciliar ecclesiology of the *societas perfecta*, I find the Council setting a new theological agenda for ecclesiology.

Without prejudice to the many other interpretations of the major ecclesiological documents of the Council, I perceive three emerging, and ultimately dominant, ideas shaping the direction of the ecclesiology articulated at the Council. These ideas primarily develop out of the Mystical Body of Christ ecclesiology that gathered momentum before the Council, and are the foundation of the communion ecclesiology that would characterize post-Vatican II theological discourse. I would describe these three leading ideas as follows.

A. Theological Foundation: Renewed Pneumatology

The centrality of the Holy Spirit to the life of the Church, recovered initially by Möhler and rediscovered in the twenty years immediately preceding the Council, inform and shape the ecclesiology of Vatican II. A renewed interest in and understanding of pneumatology serves as the critical foundation of all major documents: the renewed understanding of liturgy and the sacraments, the call to holiness of all believers, the radical and universal distribution of the charisms to all the baptized, and the Church's sacramental participation *in* the world.[23] However, while this pneumatology remains central and implicit, various aspects need to be more fully expanded, articulated, and systematized. In particular, how the Spirit actually coordinates and directs the Church's life and mission; how the Spirit relates to the hierarchy, to all believers, and to humanity, and how these groups relate to one another.[24] Furthermore, the emphasis on interpersonal "communion" and the communion between persons and communities, communities with other communities, and all of these with the divine life requires greater elaboration in regard to the dynamics of this process.

B. Dominant Image: Community

The image and language of "community" and "communion" replaces that of *societas perfecta* and other more institutional terms for the Church. This marks a preference for interpersonal over institutional categories to describe ecclesiology, as well as a tendency to interpret things like discipleship, spirituality and sanctification in social rather than individualistic terms. The image of "The People of God" provides an inclusive and catholic understanding of Church that places the institutional and bureaucratic elements of the Church in a larger perspective, and places the whole Church in a wider communal and universal context.[25] The images of the "Mystical Body" and "Body of Christ" also imply a notion of Church as community with a shared life of necessary interdependence and real diversity. That the Church exists as a "community of communities" provides a further and one of the most helpful and fecund assertions of the Council.[26] The collegial nature of the episcopacy similarly implies that the Church generally acts communally even in its leadership (this certainly qualifies the normal image one holds of "hierarchy"). The Council also attempts to more clearly delineate the relationship between the universal Church and the local or particular church. It articulates this relationship by asserting the autonomy and fullness of the local church, while insisting that the local church must always exist in relationship to and as a constitutional part of the universal Church. Nevertheless, the universal Church cannot be reduced to "the sum of its parts" but always represents the one Church of Christ in its fullest visible expression. Finally, the social and communal nature of the individual, asserted in both *Lumen Gentium* and *Gaudium et Spes*,[27] offers a compelling theological anthropology upon which to ground an interpretation of grace, ecclesiology and morality/ethics in an increasingly individualistic and nihilistic age.

Some confusion remains, as mentioned above, as to the working relationship between the terminology: sometimes communion and community are used interchangeably, and other times in the documents communion seems to describe a more profound and dynamic type of relationship than those suggested by the term community. Furthermore, that persons enter into communion with one another and with communities, and that communities enter into communion with other communities, suggests that the terms are complementary but not the same.

C. Organizing Concept: Sacramentality

The notion of sacrament and sacramentality act as a leitmotif running through all the documents, and they expand it beyond its reference to liturgy and sacraments (in a strict sense) to include the very mission of the Church and the call to Christian discipleship. From the very beginning, the Council grounds ecclesiology in the triune life of God and in the missions of the persons of the Trinity toward the world.[28] The Church herself exists as a visible manifestation of the Trinity acting in time and space. The mission of the Church extends the mission of Jesus Christ himself, namely, to proclaim and inaugurate the plan of the Father for the world. Through the action of Christ's Spirit, the Church embodies and continues Christ's mission throughout the world. The Church, therefore, exists as a sacramental sign of the reign of God. The Church preaches the reign and authenticates this preaching with its own life. This provides a principle to guide its prophetic presence in the world but also challenges it to reform its internal life to be in accord with its proclamation.

Gaudium et Spes reflects some of the implications of the Church interpreted sacramentally. That the Church discloses the presence and plan of God in human history provides the cornerstone for understanding the role of the Church in the world today. In this sense, the end or destiny of the Church and the world coincide. The Church does not limit or exhaust the presence and action of the Spirit in human history, nor does it act as the only or exclusive sign of God's presence to people and the world as a whole. Nevertheless, the Church maintains a unique place in God's design for the world, and it falls to the Church to continually discern the requirements of its sacramental function within history. The nature and concrete implications of the efficacy of the Church's sign value requires further elaboration, as does the Spirit's role in using the Church to further the Spirit's mission and illumine the minds of people living beyond the boundaries of the visible community of the Church.

Notes

1. *Vatican Council II: The Conciliar and Post Conciliar Documents,* ibid., *Sacrosanctum Concilium: The Constitution on the Sacred Liturgy* (1963) 1-36, hereafter referred to as SC.
2. For the best account in English of the day-to-day activities of the Council see *Council Daybook: Sessions 1 and 2,* edited by Floyd Anderson (Washington D.C.: National Catholic Welfare Conference, 1965), *Session 3* (1965) and *Session 4* (1966). For general reference on Vatican Council II see particularly Rynne, Xavier, *Vatican Council II* (New York: Farrar, Strauss & Giroux, 1968) and Vorgrimler, Herbert, ed., *Commentary on the Documents of Vatican II,* 5 vols. (New York: Herder & Herder, 1967-1969).
3. SC, 21ff.
4. See particularly SC, 41-42.
5. Kevin W. Irwin, "The Constitution on the Sacred Liturgy" in *Vatican II and Its Documents: An American Reappraisal,* ed. Timothy E. O'Connell, Theology and Life Series, No. 15 (Collegeville, Minnesota: Michael Glazier Books, The Liturgical Press, 1991) 16-17.
6. See in particular *Vatican Council II: The Conciliar and Post Conciliar Documents,* ed. Austin Flanerry, O.P., "Euchariticum Mysterium: Instruction on the Worship of the Eucharistic Mystery" (1967) 100-136; "Indulgentiarum Doctrina: Apostolic Constitution on the Revision of Indulgences" (1967) 62-79, especially chap. 2: "The Communion of Saints"; chap. 3: "The Church Applies the Fruits of Christ's Redemption," 66-69; and "Cenam Paschalem: General Instruction on the Roman Missal" (1970) 154-205.
7. *Council Daybook, Session 3,* 299.
8. Ibid, 303-304.
9. See Hamer, 45ff.
10. Obviously, I see a strong connection here between the thought of Hamer on this terminology as outlined earlier.
11. This compares to one vote on chapter 1, four votes on chapter 2, and one vote each for chapters 4 and 5. This chapter also recorded the highest number of negative votes—ranging from 11 to 1364—with a number of the amendments recording negative votes from a consistent minority of 200–300. *Council Daybook, Session 3,* 3-10, 31-33, 121-123.
12. See particularly the speech by Pope Paul VI, *Council Daybook, Session 3,* pp. 6-10.
13. On November 16, 1964, in response to continuing questions put forward both on the floor and within the commissions themselves, the doctrinal commission formally decided to attach a "modi" or explanatory note to the third chapter of the constitution. The primary purpose of this note seems to be to define the terms "college" and "communion." The definitions follow. "The word 'college' is not taken in the strictly juridical sense, that is, as a group of equals who transfer their powers to their chairman, but as a permanent body whose form and authority is to be ascertained from revelation. For this reason it is explicitly said about the twelve apostles ... that Our Lord constituted them 'as a college or permanent group' " (*Vatican II: The Conciliar and Post-Conciliar Documents,* 424, para. 1). "Communion ... is not to be understood as some vague sort of goodwill, but as something organic which calls for a juridical structure as well as being

enkindled by charity. The commission, therefore, agreed, almost unanimously, on the wording 'in hierarchical communion' " (*Ibid*, 425, para. 2).

14. Ibid. The text does not actually articulate or clarify the conditions under which a pope can teach infallibly. In this sense, Vatican II fails to dispel the vagueness of Vatican I on the actual use of this charism.

15. The primary reason for this decision seems to have been the ecumenical thrust of the Council and a concern by many of the council fathers to avoid over-emphasizing the place of Mary in Roman Catholic theology. As a separate schema, the text on Mary evidently over-emphasized the place of Mary in the economy of salvation. By placing this statement about Mary in the context of the Church, the council fathers were actually able to articulate the role of Mary in a more adequate and ecumenically acceptable way. To read the discussions that took place on the floor of the council, see *The Council Daybook*, 15-25.

16. See particularly LG, 56.

17. *Vatican Council II: The Conciliar and Post-Conciliar Documents*, 452-473. Hereafter referred to as UR.

18. The use of this term "subsists" does seem to act as refinement and commentary on the term "subsists" as used in LG, 8.

19. This document also advances the work of Congar, as cited earlier, by freeing the charisms of the laity from the direct control of the hierarchy. The laity share directly in the apostolate and not derivatively through the administration of the hierarchy.

20. *Vatican Council II: The Conciliar and Post-Conciliar Documents*, 799-812. Also known as (in English), *Declaration on Religious Liberty*. Hereafter referred to DH.

21. John E. Linnan, C.S.V., "Declaration on Religious Liberty," *Vatican II and Its Documents: An American Reappraisal*, 167-169.

22. Quoting from LG, 8.

23. See particularly, LG, 2, 7, 8, 13, 15, 16, 39-44; GS, 7-11, 22, 26-27, 31-32; AA.

24. Compare for instance, LG 20-22 with LG, 39-44, and GS 22.

25. This becomes, I believe, the underlying and operating principle of *Gaudium et Spes*.

26. LG, 23.

27. See especially LG, 7, and GS, 23ff.

28. LG, 1ff.

Chapter 3

Understanding the Triad
that Creates Communion

Introduction

Beginning Catholic school immediately after the close of Vatican II, I never had the opportunity to learn the revered (or infamous) Baltimore Catechism, as I stated earlier. If I had, I surely would have learned formulas and details about dogmas and doctrines that had been passed down through the centuries and accounted for the treasury of the Catholic tradition. Instead, from the first through the eighth grade we primarily learned about scripture: the history underlying it, its central stories, main characters, dominant themes, and the many ethical implications that it had for our daily lives. That is not to say that we were never exposed to any dogma or doctrine, but rather that all our exposure to the tradition was seen through the prism of the Bible. Our doctrinal formation unsystematically reflected on four fundamental dimensions of Catholic thought: God as Trinity, the Incarnation, the sacraments, and Christian ethics/morality. Maybe, even without knowing it or at least fully understanding it, my teachers were enacting the very first paragraph of *Lumen Gentium* by opening up the great mysteries of the Tradition to the faithful through the light of scripture.

What emerged for me from this was a deep quandary: How could God be a Trinity? What could this possibly mean? I could understand and believe the rest of the story—the Incarnation, the sacraments, Mary—all of it; but the Trinity seemed to connote a strange and impenetrable mystery. I realized that this doctrine could not just be one idea or proposition besides many others, one more painting in the immense art museum called the Catholic Tradition. My early intuition was that the whole edifice rested on the viability and credibility of this bedrock claim about the nature of God and God's life in relation to us. Unfortunately, my early education was limited to unveiling the mystery of God. It did not actually help me penetrate more deeply this profound revelation always hovering just above or around the scriptures we so arduously studied.

Unwittingly, my own innocent intellectual struggle paralleled the wider theological and ideological revolution under way in the Catholic Church as a whole. At the center of this Copernican revolution (as I described it earlier) was precisely this radically new emphasis on the dogma of the Trinity. This is not to say that the Trinity had been absent from Catholic thought and doctrinal definition over the preceding centuries. On the contrary, it was a standard part of every theological, liturgical, and canonical formula defined, promulgated, or proposed throughout the history of the Church. But it often tended to be merely *included*—an addendum that completed an orthodox statement or proposal that had already been formulated, sometimes without even taking the Trinity into consideration. The Constitutions of Vatican II, however, made the Trinity the central and defining core around which every other dimension of life and practice was to be interpreted and understood.

The Council, called mainly to discuss matters internal to the life of the Church, realized that no adequate interpretation of its life and mission could take place outside of the divine life and plan for all creation, revealed in the missions of the Son and the Spirit. In other words, all of creation and the Church itself could only be adequately understood in light of the outpouring of the triune divine love of the Father, Son, and Holy Spirit. This reality had to serve as the starting point, context, and goal of all theological reflection and practical planning for matters internal and external to ecclesial life. The Trinity, therefore, serves as more than just the major theological topic of the Council or even the main source of other theological discourse; it is really the canvas on which the vast landscape of Vatican II was portrayed. The Trinity penetrates and runs through the documents like a vast river with many tributaries, streams, and trickling branches. It was the recovery, renewal, and reinterpretation of this most foundational dogma (as Congar and others realized) that made the Second Vatican Council possible.

With the spotlight recast brightly on the central character of theology, another primary player began to emerge slowly from the shadows. The Holy Spirit, consigned to a secondary role for centuries and almost overshadowed altogether by the Counter-Reformation, appears on the main stage at Vatican II. Given the centrality of the roles that missions of the persons of the Trinity play in organizing and coordinating God's plan of redemption in general and the Church in particular, the Holy Spirit assumes a dynamic and leading role in each. The New Testament reveals that the mission of the Holy Spirit, though wider than the boundaries of the visible Church, serves as the source of growth and unity of the Church. Jesus Christ gives the Spirit to the Church as the guarantee of the continuation on earth and in history of his life and work—literally his body—for the service of the redemption and salvation of all humankind. Vatican II, therefore, in its reflection, had to dwell in a new and particularly sustained way on the Holy Spirit and the Spirit's unique relationship with the Church and her members.

In this part of the book, I will further explore the component parts of the "triad" that create genuine communion: pneumatology, community, and sacrament. Based on the documents of Vatican II, the Trinitarian backdrop that underlies all orthodox theology and contemporary scholarship in each of these component parts, I will offer a fuller understanding of these significant realities.

Part I: The Holy Spirit—The Giver of Life

The Holy Spirit in Scripture

In the opening chapters of the book of Genesis, we see that part of the divine life that we will call the Holy Spirit acting in two significant but different ways. The Hebrew word that is translated into English as spirit is *ruah*. *Ruah* literally means "breath" or "breathing into" and connotes a life source that can be transmitted to something or someone. It can also refer to a strong, rushing desert wind that carries a great deal of force or power. In Genesis 1:2 the *ruah* of God is "moving over the waters" of chaos and darkness out of which God creates the heavens and earth in seven days. In Genesis 2:7, God creates a man from the soil of the earth and *breathes* life into him, and the man begins *breathing* on his own. So the divine *ruah* serves as both agent and catalyst of the whole of creation and as a special and profoundly intimate link between human beings and God.

Throughout the Hebrew Scriptures the divine *ruah* acts in this dual way: as a transformative force at work in the world and as a personal link to the divine life empowering new religious consciousness, authentic prophecy, and creative interpretation of the will of God.[1] This general understanding of *ruah* that pervades the primary texts of the Hebrew Scriptures comes to a unique fulfillment in the Jewish writings known as the Wisdom literature. In this body of texts the Hellenic idea of Wisdom is brought into such a close approximation with the *ruah*, or rather its Greek equivalent *pneuma*, that the two are almost identified or at least seen to have the same action and effect. Here Wisdom, personified as a woman, helps human beings penetrate to the heart of things, opening up the complexity and mystery of life to those who trust and follow her. Entering into this new relationship with lady wisdom offers the person new vision and a new critical frame of reference from which to judge reality more genuinely and truly. This suggests that the relationship with the *pneuma*, like that

with lady wisdom, is a profoundly intimate and transformative experience that brings the person into a new level of
conscious awareness about the world and about his or her relationship with God. It also gives us our first personal biblical
metaphor for the third person of the Trinity: that of a beau-
tiful and wise woman mentor, who attracts us and guides us
into ever-deeper realms of knowledge and love.

In the New Testament the *pneuma* is particularly present in
the Letters of Paul, the Acts of the Apostles, and the Gospel of
John. In the Synoptic Gospels, Jesus is always depicted as the
one with the fullness of the *pneuma* and the one who shares his
own *pneuma* with his disciples after his death and resurrection.
Jesus' own life is not seen as ancillary to that of the divine
pneuma, nor vice versa. But in all narrative accounts, Jesus' life
represents or signifies what the human life open to the transforming power of the *pneuma* might look like in general. The
Gospels are actually written later than the Pauline letters and
serve as an attempt to remember the life and teaching of Jesus
in light of the Paschal Mystery that is the true center of each
gospel proclamation. The Pauline texts, written explicitly in
light of and in reference to the Paschal Mystery, offer us a
more direct understanding of the pneumatolgy of the New
Testament. Similarly, the Acts of the Apostles, as a kind of
record of the *pneuma's* direct work in building up the Body of
Christ as the final stage of the Paschal Mystery, give witness to
the unique pattern of the *pneuma's* "working relationship"
with the Christian communities.

Pneuma *in Paul*

Paul has a privileged place among New Testament writers
for two reasons: He personally saw the resurrected Jesus (probably the only New Testament writer to have done so), and he
reflects in considerable detail its theological significance in the
light of his own experience and in that of others, which had
been directly communicated to him. In his surviving letters,
Paul's theological vision develops contextually and pastorally
rather than systematically. Nevertheless, he demonstrates a

remarkable level of coherence in his religious vision and under-standing of the meaning of Jesus Christ and the Paschal Mystery. Paul's pneumatology, therefore, arose in tandem with his Christology as a response to very specific doctrinal and pastoral problems that developed in the communities that he founded.

One of the earliest and most significant texts of Christological and pneumatological importance is 1 Corin-thians 15. This text evidently develops as a response to the fact that some members of the Corinthian community doubt the possibility of Christ's bodily resurrection. In response to this, Paul underscores that Jesus not only died but was "buried," and that he rose and "appeared to not only Cephas and the twelve but to a whole host of other brothers and sisters, some five hundred in all" (including Paul himself) (vv. 5–6). This means that Jesus' resurrection was not a private encounter or revelation shared by few, but literally represents the shared faith and experience of the first community of Christians. It is this experience that authenticates the good news that they proclaim, including the one about the bodily resurrection. So any doubts about the resurrection directly contradict the shared faith of the rest of the apostolic community. In the rest of this chapter, Paul goes on to develop a very dynamic and complex picture of Jesus' resurrection.

It is in this context that Paul makes what at first seems like an astonishing claim: through the resurrection, Jesus has "become a life-giving Spirit [*pneuma*]" (1 Cor 15:45). This assertion obviously has strong implications that need to be explored in depth. It implies that Jesus' personal transforma-tion in the *pneuma* culminated in the resurrection, because it transformed him totally, making his physical body into a pneumatic body capable of existing in an imperishable and heavenly mode of existence. This also reveals that there is both a vital and functional identity of life between the risen Christ and the *pneuma* of God. It is vital because Christ shares fully in the divine pneumatic life in a unique and distinct way, which implies that both are equally part of God's single plan for salvation. There is a functional identity because both act in ways that are "life-giving" and sanctifying for those who put their faith in God's saving power acting through the Paschal Mystery.

This same rhetorical strategy is seen in 2 Corinthians 3:15–18. Here again Paul refers to the risen Christ in relation to the *pneuma*:

> Now the Lord is the *pneuma*, and where the *pneuma* of the Lord is, there is freedom. And all of us, with unveiled faces, seeing the glory of the Lord as though reflected in a mirror, are being transformed into the same image from one degree of glory to another; for this comes from the Lord, the *pneuma*. (2 Cor 3:17–18)

Paul implies that there is a *functional identity* between Jesus and the *pneuma* such that wherever the *pneuma* of God is present and acting, so is the risen Christ. But there is more than a functional identity, there is a *vital identity*: whoever possesses the *pneuma* of God possesses the risen life of Christ. By vital identity I am implying an essential or what we would refer to in philosophy as an "ontological" relationship. The *pneuma* of God transforms believers into the "image" of Christ, reflecting back his glory. These believers are growing "from one degree of glory to another," meaning that the resurrection offers progressive and intensive growth and transformation in the *pneuma*. The new life initiated by the Paschal Mystery is a historical process that is continued through the power of the *pneuma* grounded in the vital identity of life shared by the *pneuma* and the risen Christ.

Throughout the Bible the *ruah/pneuma* functions as the divine principle of empowering, saving enlightenment. By asserting a functional and vital identity between the risen Christ and the divine *pneuma*, Paul establishes that in the encounter with the risen Lord we receive the Spirit in a powerful and transforming way, and vice versa. This experience gives believers the authority and hope to testify to the saving power of the resurrection. It also means that a personal encounter with the Spirit connects us directly with the Paschal Mystery and allows us to share in its fruits. Paul offers us a view of the work of the *pneuma* that is liberating rather than controlling, cooperative rather than overpowering. The *pneuma* helps us not only to see but *desire* to see God.

This understanding of the Paschal Mystery is brought to a kind of systematic presentation in Paul's Letter to the Romans. Throughout this text Paul reflects on the saving mystery of Christ's death and resurrection and its literal and practical implications for believers and all of humanity. This reflection comes to a crescendo in chapter 8.

> You are no longer ruled by your desires, but by God's Spirit, who lives in you. People who do not have the Spirit of Christ in them do not belong to him. But Christ lives in you. So you are alive because God has accepted you, even though your bodies must die because of sins. Yet God raised Jesus to life! God's Spirit now lives in you, and he will raise you to life by his Spirit. . . . Only those people who are led by God's Spirit are his children. God's Spirit does not make us slaves who are afraid of him. Instead, we become his children and call him "Abba." God's Spirit makes us sure that we are his children. His Spirit lets us know that together with Christ we will be given what God has promised. We will also share in the glory of Christ, because we have suffered with him. (Rom 8:9–17)

Paul presents an understanding of human existence transformed through the Paschal Mystery in the power of the *pneuma* that can only be described as a "mutual indwelling": Christians in Christ, Christ in Christians, Christians in the *pneuma*, the *pneuma* in Christians. Through the *pneuma* we are incorporated literally and given a share in Christ's risen life and conformed morally to him. This pneumatic transformation enables righteous living that manifests God's presence. It also literally gives us a new history in that we take on the story of Christ himself: Christ's story and relationships becomes ours. This means that we enter into the family of God in a radically new way, a way that gives us direct access to the Father and that unites us with all God's children who have been adopted in Christ. The mutual indwelling affected by this transformation implies then an added indwelling of Christians in one another.

The implications of the social and communal dimensions of pneumatic transformation are most thoroughly explored by Paul in Romans 12–14 and in 1 Corinthians 12 (and will be investigated in the next chapter on community). In both instances he examines the Christian community in terms of the inter-relationships between the parts of a body. He insists that the fullness of the *pneuma* can only be experienced in community, and never in some kind of mystical isolation. The *pneuma* builds up the community through *charismata*: gracious gifts that are particular instances of *charis* or God's saving activity (grace). It is the interrelating and mutual sharing of these *charismata* that make community possible and the *pneuma* fully manifest. The *pneuma's* manifestation is ultimately the manifestation of the presence of Christ; it is the sharing of the *charismata* that makes us the Body of Christ. Furthermore, the *pneuma* links up each community historically/spatio-temporally with other communities of faith in the worldwide Body of Christ. In chapter 8 of Romans, Paul goes on to explain how the *pneuma* connects each community into the universal community, and ultimately ties the whole universe into the life of God.

A final important dimension of Paul's understanding of the unique mission of the divine *pneuma* is revealed in 1 Corinthians 2:10–16:

> God's Spirit has shown you everything. His Spirit finds out everything, even what is deep in the mind of God. You are the only one who knows what is in your own mind, and God's Spirit is the only one who knows

what is in God's mind. But God has given us his Spirit. That is why we do not think the same way that people of this world think. That is also why we can recognize the blessings that God has given us. . . . People who are guided by the *pneuma* can make all kinds of judgments, but they cannot be judged by others. The scriptures ask, "Has anyone ever known the thoughts of the Lord or given him advice?" But we think as Christ does.

For Paul the *pneuma* is the very mind of God, and therefore to be personally transformed in and enlightened by the *pneuma* is to be drawn into the divine life in a totally unique and extraordinary way. In the power of the *pneuma* we know the depths of our own conscious dynamism, and we also know of God's saving intention for us and all humanity. The fruit of this type of knowledge is hope and complete trust in God's providence (as opposed to skepticism and fear). Jesus incarnates the mind of God; he is the spoken Word that gives us concrete knowledge of what we need to know about God and God's plan for our world. The *pneuma* as the mind of God transforms us so that we can take on the mind of Christ and thereby serve the plan of God as ongoing part of Jesus Christ's own life and mission.

Luke-Acts-Pentecost

Although we know little about the author of the community being written to, we know a great deal about Luke's intention in writing the Gospel. In his prologue to both the Gospel and Acts (Lk 1:1–4; Acts 1:1–5) he states that he wants to write a two-volume study of the origins of Christianity. The first volume recounts Jesus' proclamation of the kingdom, the second the Christian community's proclamation of the risen Christ. Thus, the first volume is about the life, message, and Paschal Mystery of Jesus Christ, while the second treats the coming of the *pneuma* and its life and activity through the Christian community. There is a parallel in the first volume between the movement of Jesus from Galilee to Jerusalem and the movement of the proclamation from Jerusalem to Rome. The collapse of Jerusalem (figuratively) and Judaism (literally) with the execution of Jesus signals the birth and expansion of the gospel throughout the world with the resurrection and the sending of the *pneuma*.

The first Pentecost Event in the Acts of the Apostles leads to a series of "pentecosts"—events that are still going on to this day. We can clearly see two, one major and one minor.

Major Pentecost Event:
1) Acts 2:1–40 — Pentecost Event and Preaching
2) Acts 2:41 — Conversion of Hearers
3) Acts 2:42–47 — Community:

They devoted themselves to the apostles' teaching and fellowship, to breaking of bread and prayers. Awe came upon everyone, because many wonders and signs were being done by the apostles. All who believed were together and had all things in common; they would sell their possessions and goods and distribute the proceeds to all, as any had need. Day by day, as they spent much time together in the temple, they broke bread at home and ate their food with glad and generous hearts, praising God and having the goodwill of all people. And day by day the Lord added to their number those who were being saved.

Minor Pentecost Event:
1) Acts 4:31 — Manifestation of the transformative
        power of the *pneuma*
2) Acts 4:32–36 — Community:

Now the whole group of those who believed were of one heart and soul, and no one claimed private owner-ship of any possessions, but everything they owned was held in common. With great power the apostles gave their testimony to the resurrection of the Lord

Jesus, and great grace was upon them all. There was
not a needy person among them, for as many as owned
lands or houses sold them and brought the proceeds of
what was sold. They laid it at the apostles' feet and it
was distributed to each as any had need.

For the author of Luke/Acts the immediate response to
hearing the word through preaching and the subsequent experience of the transformative power of the *pneuma* is the formation of a radically new community (as described in Acts
2:42–47 and 4:32–36). This community is characterized by a
sharing of life and goods; it includes a literal sharing of earthly
possessions and reaches its fullness in the communion of one's
heart and mind. Thus, the *pneuma* is mediated to us through
the witness of others, especially through a transformed
community. While it is also experienced personally, the
pneuma draws the individual into the community of believers
that is literally the Body of Christ.

Another important incident reported in Acts that needs to
be examined is the story of Ananias and Sapphira (Acts
5:1–11). In this episode a married couple sell their land but lay
only part of it at the apostles' feet, holding back the rest for
their own personal use. When Peter finds out about this he
asks them how Satan has tempted them to "lie to the *pneuma*"
(v. 3). At this accusation Ananias drops dead. Later, the
Apostle confronts Sapphira with the question, "How could
you conspire to tempt the Spirit?" (v. 9). At this she too is
struck dead. Obviously this story, while odd, reflects back on
the earlier texts about the radical sharing that characterized
true pneumatic transformation and the new type of
communal living that emerged from it.

In this context, to betray or subvert the community through
selfishness is to betray God. The text further implies that the
personal willingness to share one's possessions with others
(especially those most in need) is the practical test of one's
trust in God; it is the fruit of transformation in the *pneuma*, the
authenticating mark of conversion, and the fruit of knowledge

of God. Real discipleship authenticates all revelation or knowledge about God (orthopraxis authenticates orthodoxy). Preaching the gospel must be authenticated by life, especially the life of a transformed community. So the *pneuma* also acts as judge: the *pneuma* holds the converted responsible for their authenticity and for accepting the moral consequences of their conversion.

Pneuma *and* Parakletos *in the Gospel of John*

In John's Gospel the *pneuma* inspires authentic worship of God and is the source of divine enlightenment that guides the disciples of Jesus in faithful witness to his resurrection. John also introduces the term *Parakletos* to refer to the *pneuma* in the last discourse of Jesus. This is the only place in the Fourth Gospel and in the whole of the New Testament where this term appears.[2]

In two central texts early in the Gospel, Jesus refers to the essentially pneumatic character of all authentic worship of God. To Nicodemus' inquiry about the possibility of being reborn a second time, Jesus answers in part: "Before you can enter into God's kingdom, you must be born of water and the *pneuma*. Flesh gives birth to flesh, but whatever is born of the *pneuma* is *pneuma*" (3:5–6). And later, to the Samaritan woman, Jesus proclaims:

> Yet an hour is coming and is already here when true
> worshipers will worship the Father in spirit and truth.
> Indeed, it is just such worshipers the Father seeks. God
> is spirit, and those who worship him must worship in
> spirit and truth. (4:23–24)

These texts dramatically imply that the *pneuma* designates a central reality in which both the Father and Jesus participate. To be reborn in the *pneuma* or to worship in the *pneuma* is to enter fully into the very mystery of God's own life revealed in the incarnate Christ. To truly worship as Christ does is to see the face of the Father and to gain the Wisdom of God, the truth that Jesus Christ makes real through his life, ministry, message, and passion. Jesus is "the way, the truth and the life" (14:6–7), and the *pneuma* makes his saving truth, way, and very life accessible to all those who are open to the transforming power of the *pneuma*. Once one has this saving transformation, temple worship (even at Jerusalem) and all other forms of institutional religion are rendered secondary to and at the service of authentic Christian worship.

Jesus comes to offer new life, and those who want it will be given it through his own flesh and blood and his *pneuma*, the source of all life. John alludes to this basic formula throughout the Gospel and makes it the foundation of eucharistic theology. To share in Christ's life is to share in the divine life itself in a literal and direct way.

In the course of Jesus' Last Discourse he promises that after he is gone he will send a *Parakletos* to confirm the faith of the disciples and to guide them in their post-resurrection mission. The term *Parakletos* has a rich variety of meanings and connotations. Most commonly, however, it is interpreted in legal or forensic terms. In this sense, the *Parakletos* that Jesus will send is understood to be both an attorney, who will convict the world of its guilt in rejecting Jesus, and an advocate or witness, who will come to testify with and on behalf of the disciples of Jesus who remain true to him. The activity of the *Parakletos* will be to stand by, encourage, and strengthen those who proclaim Jesus as the risen Christ.

The *Parakletos* will also teach and guide the disciples by instructing them in the light of the resurrection as to what they must now say and do in the name of Jesus. At one point in the Last Discourse Jesus promises that he will send "another *Parakletos*" (14:16), implying that Jesus himself is the first. The second *Parakletos* will come to continue and prolong the work of Jesus and to teach the disciples as Jesus himself had done, conforming them into his own likeness. John's Jesus realizes that during his lifetime he cannot teach his disciples all that they need to know, because they are unable to hear and understand it. Jesus in turn shares with the disciples only what he himself has learned from the Father. So the second *pneuma*, as the second *Parakletos*, enlightens the disciples after the resurrection of Christ with his own knowledge of the divine truth, a knowledge that he learned from the Father. This suggests that for John the *pneuma* functions as the locus of interaction between the Father and the Son and that human beings who experience the transforming power of the *pneuma* enter into a triadic relationship with the *pneuma*, the Son, and the Father. This relationship is the new life that Jesus came to bring and the salvation that he promised to all believers.

Conclusions from Paul, Luke/Acts and John

First, in Paul, Jesus mediates the divine *pneuma* to his disciples; but after Jesus' death, resurrection, and ascension the *pneuma* mediates the risen Christ to the community that has literally become his body. Secondly, the *pneuma* searches the mind of God and gives believers the mind of Christ. The *pneuma* therefore is the source of gracious enlightenment and knowledge of the Truth that Jesus incarnated and that he in turn learned from the Father. As such, the *pneuma* marks the beginning of a new creation: a new life characterized by sharing in the triune life of the Father, Son, and *pneuma* in a "mutual indwelling." This new reality literally "makes all things new" and has social, moral, and cosmic consequences. Thirdly, there is an outpouring of the *pneuma* on all believers. The sharing of the *pneuma* is what makes the community of believers into the Body of Christ. The interdependent sharing of *charismata* creates the type of authentic life that characterizes any Christian community. Finally, the moral demands of communal living are the direct consequences of the Spirit's transformative action. "To walk in the newness of life" is a literal statement that describes the type of radical personal sharing and openness to the gifts and needs of others that connotes complete trust in the providential care of the Father and the saving example of the Son's life and ministry. This implies that there is a prohibition of conduct incompatible with the mind of God as revealed in Christ (i.e., all forms of egotism and selfishness). The readiness and willingness to forgive everyone and to love even one's enemies are the practical tests of whether one has truly "put on Christ" and become a new creation.

The fullness of revelation about the *pneuma* is that it not only acts as the source of unity and sharing of gifts within each community but also as the bond uniting each particular community into the wider communion that forms the Body of Christ. This community of communities acts analogously to each particular community in that there exists a necessary sharing of gifts and needs that builds up and interrelates communities in such a way that they literally function like a body. It is the divine *pneuma* that coordinates and sustains this interaction as well as unites the entire universal community of communities with the divine life.

Pneumatology in the Theological Tradition

In the period after the New Testament, the theology of the Holy Spirit develops in tandem with the theology of the Trinity as a whole. The Trinity is primarily known to humans by its effects in history: creation, redemption, and sanctification. These effects are actually its missions—its self-motivated and directed desire to relate to and save human beings and all creation. Trinity means that there is not just one monolithic God that acts in a variety of ways but a single dynamic reality composed of distinct persons: one God as a divine community. We participate in this divine community in creation and through the presence of the one divine life in our history and individual lives that we call supernatural grace. We imitate and share in this reality through our life in communion in imitation of Jesus Christ. He is the incarnate, historical presence of this reality: one person of this divine community whose mission it was to become a divine/human person to insure our salvation. Jesus Christ comes to participate directly in our reality and to proclaim and demonstrate God's view of the world and its destiny. Jesus also comes to give us the Spirit and to inaugurate a new dimension of the Spirit's mission. The Spirit no longer acts on behalf of God only in general but actually unites human beings as the Body of Christ, gives them the mind of Jesus Christ, and puts them in the same relationship with the Father that Jesus had with him.

The Spirit who gives us God's view of things by forming us into a community that becomes Christ points us to Jesus Christ and through him to the Father. This transformation takes place at an ongoing personal and communal level. It is facilitated and empowered by personal openness to the Spirit and the personal relationship with each person of the Trinity. The Holy Spirit, therefore, inherently draws people into the triune divine community and into an authentic relationship with all the persons of the Trinity. Pneumatology necessarily implies trinitarian faith and trinitarian spirituality. Pneumatology also necessarily implies community: a participation at both divine and human levels.

Pneumatology fundamentally deals with the interrelationships between the persons of the triune community (Godhead) and the relationships between individuals, individuals and communities, and communities with the divine community. In regard to individual human beings, pneumatology is the mediation of the Trinity's relationship with each person and means that there is a distinctive and unique way in which every person relates to the divine life and the divine plan. This leads me to endorse the following important principles in pneumatology:

1) The way that we exist in God makes a difference to God.
2) The way that we exist in God makes a difference to the way that God exists in us.[3]

One of the most profound mysteries of the whole of scripture is that God, through the transformative power of the Spirit, chooses us. Purely out of love, God chooses to relate to us and to invite us into a saving relationship with him. God chooses to interact with us and to accept the consequences of our choices. Similarly, we can choose to interact or not with God and accept the consequences of either choice.

The transformative power of the Spirit makes the first contact with human beings in this interaction, but we must respond. Thus, life is an ongoing process of God's offer and our response. God continually attempts to liberate and empower us to respond positively to his offer of love and grace, but ultimately it is our choice, a choice that is neither made once and for all, nor is it obvious or simple. Life then is a project, an ongoing and continual series of choices, opportunities, habits and practices that respond to God's offer or ignore and reject it. God wants to be an active partner in our life, guiding us toward the reign of God, but we have to choose to accept this offer of divine presence and guidance. The Holy Spirit, if we desire it, acts as our first contact and as the guiding force in our full conversion into a relationship with all the persons of the Trinity. This conversion is the goal of any integral and complete spiritual journey.

The universe shares in an analogous journey. It too is involved in an ongoing and emerging process. The universe is God's project, in many ways a diffusion of God's own life. Romans, chapter 8, reminds us that the whole of creation longs for the salvation of the children of God. The Holy Spirit strives not just to reunite each individual with the divine community but to bring the entire universe back into the divine life in some kind of transformed and glorious way. The work of the Holy Spirit exceeds merely human personal dimensions of existence and is at work in all dimensions of God's creation to unify and redeem it to the full scope of God's original plan for the universe.

Pneumatology and Spirituality

The starting point of spirituality is always conversion (*metanoia*): the acceptance of a personal transformation process and an ongoing dialogue with and in the Spirit of God.

Conversion and spirituality lead to a new interpretation of one's personal life and the world as a whole. It can neither be an individualistic, self-centered quest nor a formalized and objective program without genuinely personal dimensions and diversifications. From this emerge the following characteristics of spirituality:

1) It is always communal because it is the fruit of both communal and individual, thus integral, conversion.

2) It concerns the whole person: both body and soul, spiritual/affective and ethical/moral life.

3) It is a pattern of ongoing conversion that takes on a unique configuration of symbols, practices, etc., depending on the persons involved, historical and cultural situations, the theological and philosophical foundations of the movement that gives rise to the pattern of conversion.

4) Spiritualities give rise to "schools" or organized/institutionalized communities of ongoing conversion that usually have a shared common story or stories and shared vision of the future. They also usually have a specific founder whose initial conversion experience is idealized and imitated.

Within the Christian community there are many different spiritualities and patterns of living out Christian conversion. Religious life in the West, for example, is a particular expression of the spirituality it derived from the many that developed in the two-thousand-year history of Christian civilization. Conversion and the articulation of conversion always take place in some cultural context: some frame of reference that is limited and emerging. This cultural context can be converted or subverted, or can convert or subvert the community and individual.

Spirituality includes Christian prayer and worship, because they are essential dimensions of any integrally converted Christian life. But it connotes more than simply prayer or prayer forms. Spirituality describes the action of the Holy Spirit in the entire range of human life and in the life of the Christian community. It thus denotes the project of a life lived in response to God's offer of a divine, triune relationship. Any authentic Christian spirituality must be fully grounded in a pneumatology that situates the spiritual journey in terms of ongoing holistic adult conversion and a fully Trinitarian context.

Pneumatology and the Charisms

"To each is given the manifestation of the Spirit for the common good" (1 Cor 12:7). Part of any spiritual community, and hence any spirituality, is the sharing of the charisms that create community and manifest the individual dimension of each person's relationship with the Spirit. The sharing of gifts is what makes a given community truly Christ (since the community is a sign of Christ only when it has the fullness of the Spirit, and this is the case only when there is complete sharing of gifts). Paul refers to the Church as the Body of Christ in both a literal and analogous sense.[4] In the analogous sense, the community is like a body or an orchestra. There are no extra or unnecessary parts, no membership apart from full membership. For Paul there can be no genuine community without a sharing of individual charisms by all members. The Spirit coordinates and animates the community by both discerning and calling forth these gifts. This process of discernment then serves as one of the primary tasks of the community and implies that it can only continue to exist as a community through this activity.

Personal charisms are a combination of the natural talents and dispositions of the person and the needs of the community. For this reason conversion is necessary, because it is foundational for many of the charisms. Not all gifts, talents, and abilities are Spirit-given charisms. Likewise, there is no universal and exhaustive list of charisms. The needs develop as the community emerges, and the charisms emerge depending on the people in the community.

Trust is the foundation of community, and unconditioned sharing and willingness to receive the gifts of others is the fruit of conversion and fundamental requirement for community. Refusing to share one's gifts with the community or a communal refusal to discern the gifts, constitutes a sin against the Holy Spirit. The same is true of a communal or institutional paralysis that concentrates all the gifts in the hands of a few, inhibits the sharing of gifts, or does not respond to the needs that have arisen in the community by calling forth new gifts. This can ultimately destroy the community, because there is no basis for communal life apart from the sharing of gifts; it is what differentiates a community from, for example, a club, clique, or therapy group.

Each Christian community also has a unique charism or charisms that it is meant to share with the wider Christian community, thus enabling the possibility of a universal community of communities. This specific charism is often closely identified with the particular community's spirituality. It is a unique configuration of elements, often grounded in the life a particular person or group of persons, that creates the language, symbols, concrete goals, and fundamental orientation and interpretive framework for its members. This charism is usually tied to a certain narrative tradition that informs and shapes it at an imaginative and pre-rational level; a story not identical to the charism but necessary and essential to it. A charism is a prism through which a given community will interpret reality and shape its corporate behavior. It gives the group ethical imperatives and focuses the scope of its concerns and activities.

Charism always implies building up the larger community. (Even the universal Church ultimately participates in the wider universal community that she is meant to build up through her gifts and from which she also receives gifts.) Identifying and discerning the charism of a particular community is not just a historical process; it is a contemporary sociological and religious project as well. The process of discerning a charism is really the process of inculturation: creating an emerging community that is actively engaged in a particular cultural context. This can be very difficult, because it presumes that the community is composed of people who are part of an ongoing communal conversion process, where there is a sharing and discerning of gifts and a life that has been adapted to articulate and respond to the needs of the wider community in which the group is situated. Most importantly, the community must be able to identify the imaginative and pre-rational side of its spirituality. Identifying a charism is really taking on a new communal imagination of seeing and interpreting the world in a new way. A charism is necessary to constitute a community, because every community exists as part of some wider community, and so we discern a communal charism in a similar way as we discern an individual charism or charisms in each particular community.

Conclusion: The Work of the Spirit in the Church and the World

A. The "Work" of the Spirit

The Spirit of God, at work in human history since the dawn of creation and present in a particular and profound way in the life of Jesus Christ, takes on a new role and purpose at Pentecost. The divine Spirit becomes the Spirit of the risen Christ uniting people in his memory and preparing all creation for the coming reign of God he inaugurated. The Church represents the effect of the Spirit's mission.

1. The Spirit Creates

The Spirit creates the Church, constituting it as the new Body of Christ. As such, the Church embodies the risen Christ in history by working for the coming kingdom in word and deed as Jesus did in his own lifetime, thereby serving as the sign of God's love for humanity. The Spirit animates and coordinates this body by building up and coordinating its internal life through a distribution of gifts to all the members of the community. These shared charisms unite the community and literally enable it to function as a body (analogous to a person) in history. The Spirit guides the community in its witness of life and uses it as an efficacious instrument to announce and bring about the kingdom of God. The connection between the manifestation of the Spirit and the formation of the Christian community can be seen most dramatically in the Acts of the Apostles (Acts 2:1–47 and 4:31–37). A common life of prayer, mutual sharing of gifts and resources, and a "oneness" in heart and mind characterize the communities that result from the outpouring of the Spirit on the apostolic group.

2. The Spirit Unites

The Spirit serves to unite each individual or community into a community of communities, and all of these into the people of God. The Spirit also unites the people of God to all those communities throughout time and space that work to realize the final loving plan of God for the universe. Ultimately, the Spirit works to unite all God's creation together and bring it to a supreme unity with the divine life itself. For this reason the Spirit not only serves as the bond of love and unity between the Church and Jesus Christ, but as the unifying force drawing all creation into a final encounter with its creator, the triune God.

3. The Spirit Transforms

The Spirit actually accomplishes this unifying function by transforming both persons and communities over time into the unique people and communities that God created them to be. Central, then, to understanding the work of the Spirit is understanding the Spirit's role in conversion (*metanoia*): the graced transformation of persons and communities into the image of God. The Spirit serves as the source of enlightenment and insight to those persons who seek to understand and interpret their lives in a more thorough and comprehensive way than "conventional wisdom" dictates. The Spirit works to draw these individuals into ever deeper levels of personal awareness and self-consciousness that arouse in them the pressing and heartfelt need for "something more" in their lives. At the same time the Spirit draws the person into communities, which serve as a "matrix of grace" offering the individual healing and growth in all the major dimensions of their personality. These communities also offer the person a comprehensive vision of reality and a genuine life plan, which combine their own inherent and natural talents and aspirations with plans and goals wider than themselves and greater than their own personal aspirations. When these communities have themselves been transformed by the Spirit into communities striving to attain the ultimate unity and fulfillment of the universe, they exist as explicitly religious communities and work in various degrees to realize the plan of God for human history.

4. The Spirit Incorporates

The Christian Church exists as a living part of the people of God and represents a conscious choice by the Spirit to create a community that prolongs and extends the life and ministry of Jesus Christ. The Spirit incorporates members into this community through the same process of conversion that the Spirit offers to all human beings in one way or another throughout history. By becoming a member of the Christian community, a person receives a special and shared revelation of God's plan for the universe, thereby making that person a self-conscious participant in this divine process. As such, Christian conversion signifies one of the most important, but also most difficult, forms of human religious conversion. Because of the special relationship the Christian communities have with the risen Christ, and the special knowledge and power that this relationship enables, the Christian community bears a special responsibility for conscientiously and decisively working for the kingdom of God.

5. The Spirit Judges

The Divine Spirit not only acts as the animating Spirit of the community in a particularly powerful way but as its conscience and judge. The Spirit holds the Christian community to a special degree of integrity, because God intends it to serve as a special sign and source—a sacrament—of the kingdom in human history.

Communion Pneumatology

Implied in all the preceding has been an attempt to offer a theological reflection on the two fundamental constitutions of the Church: *Lumen Gentium* and *Gaudium et Spes*. Both are characterized by radically pneumatological foundations that move them beyond classic Church/world distinctions and into a dynamic communal relationship not only within the Church but also with the rest of humanity and with its deepest yearnings and greatest suffering. The Constitutions, therefore, rest on a new type of theological outlook (Communion Pneumatology) that must now be seen as normative for not only ecclesiology but other aspects of dogmatic theology.

A. The Spirit in the Church

All of this implies the need for a very vital and vigorous understanding of pneumatology within the Christian community. Because the Christian community knows both the plan of God and the abiding presence of God's Spirit leading and directing it in the fulfillment of this plan, this community has a special responsibility to listen to and respect the promptings of the Spirit in the ongoing life of the community. Any Christian community bears the special responsibility to respond obediently and efficaciously to the will of the Spirit. This implies that each community allow the full distribution of the charisms as the Spirit wills and that it be willing to grow and adapt based on the changing and developing contexts in which it finds itself. The community must trust that the Spirit will lead it faithfully in the memory of Jesus' own saving actions and atoning acts, but also that the Spirit will guide the community into the future according to the needs of the universal process that the Spirit oversees and directs. This means that the community must radically open itself up to receive new insights from the Spirit, and shape and reform its life by interpreting the actions of the Spirit in history and in its own life. This understanding of and confidence in the work of the Spirit implies that the community should consider no single practice, habit, or organizational structure as unchange-able or unalterable in principle, regardless of its origins or the length of its observance. The Spirit always remains free to introduce new ideas, forms of communal life, ministry and organization into any Christian community, not contrary to the will of Jesus Christ, but precisely as the continuation of his saving action on behalf of the kingdom.

B. The Spirit in the World

Because of the relationship to the Spirit, the Church also enjoys a special relationship to the rest of the world. In this context we can understand the teaching of *Gaudium et Spes* that calls upon the Church to serve the world as an "inter-preter" and guide, explaining and conveying the world's deepest longings and aspirations. This, I believe, constitutes what *Gaudium et Spes* calls "reading the signs of the times." It also offers us an insight into the sacramentality unique to the Christian community (to be discussed in more detail below). Each Christian community, and the community of all of them together, stand as a sign, a living witness, and an instrument of the Spirit in the process of guiding the world into the fullness of the plan of God. Any Christian community can serve as a sacrament of the kingdom of God by offering its own life as a sign, a glimpse, and a foretaste of the kingdom. Each commu-nity can likewise block or obstruct the kingdom by acting in ways that discourage, hurt, or oppress people and thereby frus-trate the very power of the Spirit whom they possess.

This type of pneumatology, therefore, calls the community to be aware of and open to the manifold and numerous ways in which the Spirit is working efficaciously outside of the visible Christian community. The Spirit works converting individ-uals and communities everywhere in the world in a myriad of ways, and continually draws all human beings into an emerging life of unity and reconciliation. The Church must always humbly interpret itself and its own role in the context of the mystery of this divine process.

Part II: Community—"Members One of Another"

"We, though many, are one body in Christ, and individually members one of another" (Rom 12:5). This single Pauline insight, taken as literally as possible, underlies the central anthropological presupposition of any communion ecclesiology. We human beings are deeply interconnected and interrelated. Our very individuality is rooted in our communal existence, and only there can we become fully ourselves. Paul understood this dimension of human experience and explained it through the metaphor of the human body. Each human being has a unique existence as a member of a complex community that functions like a body—without the individual parts the body would be deficient or die; without the whole body the single parts could not have any independent life or identity (Rom 12; 1 Cor). The Gospel of John describes this profound communion (*koinonia* in Greek) through the metaphor of the vine and the branches. A branch apart from the vine withers and dies, but the vine without any branches cannot bear fruit (Jn 15). Furthermore, genuine human life, according to the Gospel of John, can only be lived in a communal context.[5] The Constitutions of the Church also presume this kind of social anthropology as the basis of all reality (see especially GS 12–24).

This understanding of the individual's relationship with the community has its critics. In fact, community and the social dimension of human experience is one of the most misunderstood realities of modern life and contemporary experience. To adequately understand the Church, and the idea of communion, it is imperative to develop a clear meaning of community itself, and particularly of the relationship between the community and the individual.

Understanding the Conditions for Genuine Community:
The Philosophy of Josiah Royce

I offer an analysis of the thought of the U.S. philosopher Josiah Royce (1855–1916), because I consider him as a resource for critical reflection on a number of the issues that arise from the theological investigation of an ecclesiology of communion. Josiah Royce joined the Harvard faculty as an instructor in 1882 and remained there as a professor of philosophy until his death in 1916. Royce created a philosophical and religious account of human experience that attempted, successfully in my estimation, to present an interpretation of the world that united the individual with the community, the particular with the universal, the human with the divine, while maintaining the genuine autonomy and integrity of each. Royce presented a metaphysical account of human experience grounded in both logical and empirical (or "social" as he called it) analysis that offered a viable and rich alternative to the many forms of idealism, materialism, and therapeutic individualism that dominated the philosophical and cultural milieu of his time.[6]

Josiah Royce developed his mature philosophy around three central or leading ideas: Spirit, community, and the interpretation of signs. Independent of any specifically ecclesiological concerns (he was not a theologian and did not belong to any particular Christian denomination), Royce investigated the metaphysical problem of "the one and the many" in a particularly helpful way. His metaphysical and practical insights into these three areas present contemporary Roman Catholic theologians with a unique opportunity to broaden and clarify their investigations into the reality of communion. His communal/social account of human knowing and anthropology, and his metaphysical insights into the divine human relationship, both endorse and help clarify the most fundamental assertions of Vatican II.

Communities of Interpretation as Foundational

The work of Josiah Royce suggests that an infinite series of interrelated and overlapping "communities of interpretation" compose what we call the world. This implies that human minds exist as inherently interconnected to one another and that proper interpretation (to which all mature minds strive) requires more than one mind. Knowledge results from a dialogue of minds, and this dialogue remains necessary to know anything and to engender any action. A community of interpretation connects us to the rest of reality, because interpreting signs functions as a fundamental human conscious process. People and their lives emerge out of this process of interpretation.

To know any reality, therefore, we must enter into a community of interpretation at some level, since genuine knowledge can only be conveyed in a community where ongoing dialogue takes place. This understanding of reality implies that individual persons can only achieve full humanity and full autonomy by creating, choosing, and nurturing social bonds. Full individuality comes when we acknowledge our interconnectedness and choose to be faithful to it. Over against the American tendency to insist on "atomic" individualism (i.e., becoming autonomous through breaking social bonds and by opting for immediate personal self-interest to any form of enduring commitment), the gospel, and subsequent theological and philosophical reflection upon it, asserts that human beings exist ultimately and profoundly as "persons-in-community." The most fundamental issue that an individual faces in his or her life, then, becomes finding and fully belonging to a genuine and life-giving community of interpretation.

Characteristics of a Genuine Community

In Royce's view there will always exist varying qualities of communal life. Over time a community can unite more fully but also disintegrate. Moreover, not all communities can be considered genuine; they can be destructive as well as salvific. The difference ultimately lies in their goal, and in their ability and willingness to foster a genuine sharing of life among their members over an extended period of time. In this sense, groups with very limited, narrowly self-serving or mean-spirited goals will always fail to fulfill the personal potential of individuals and will tend to degenerate into a self-destructive, violent chaos over time. Likewise, communities with good ends that experience institutional paralysis, substituting short-term and self-serving actions for long-term goals, will generally fail to achieve their purpose and eventually become false and inauthentic.

Elements of Community

A. Doctrine of the Two Levels of Reality: "Sacred Pair"

Given the above criteria, what insures that a community is authentic and genuine? Royce grounds his mature under-standing of community on his conviction that there exist two basic levels of reality or two types of things in the universe: individuals and communities. This denotes a "sacred pair" upon which the whole order of the universe is based.[7] He insists that a genuinely and loyally united community is no mere aggregate of otherwise detached individuals but a person in a perfectly literal sense.[8] Similarly, he defines an individual person as a community.[9] Any life rendered coherent by a choice of a plan of action and constituted by a common past, present, and future, where the past is interpreted to the future through the present and is interpreted through specific deeds and actions, exists as both a community and a person. The task remains to show how these two levels relate to one another as distinct but necessarily connected realities and how any type of community at all (whether that be the individual, the community, or the universe) functions.

This distinction allows Royce to truly grasp the reality of individuality. Royce asserts the two levels of reality by appealing to human experience. We in fact do experience

ourselves as individuals in at least three ways: 1) our bodies
and their direct sensory perceptions are unique; 2) our minds
and their strains of conscious thought are not directly accessible through intuition to any other mind; 3) our voluntary
decisions and the deeds which follow from them are our own.[10]
On the other hand, Royce argues that we do not experience
ourselves as individualistic monads, that is, as wholly separate
and discreet units of reality that only incidentally or acciden-
tally relate to one another. We commonly experience a
profound unity and interconnectedness with many other
people. Royce points to the many types of social cooperation
that bring into existence the language, customs, and religions
that make our own individual consciousness possible. He sees
these as proof of the existence of an underlying unity we
participate in, although it acts autonomously.

Collective groups have minds of their own and tend to
develop a type of shared life that cannot be identified with any
single individual. Collective groups, in fact, transcend all of
the individuals who share in them.[11] Royce calls these types of
interdependent groups "communities" and distinguishes
them from the modern ideologies of collectivism. He describes
"collectives" as soulless organizations that treat their members
as things and not as persons. Communities, on the other hand,
respect and appreciate the autonomy and individuality of
their members, while uniting them in common beliefs and
activities. Fundamental human experience shows that a
community, a social reality, can and often does work in and
through the individual.

For Royce, therefore, I am *both* an individual and a community. When fully mature I live at two distinct but interrelated
forms of consciousness wherein both forms remain fundamentally interdependent on one another. Royce believes that I, the
individual, can only become fully autonomous by being genuinely loyal to some community; a "mere" individual has not
achieved full humanity. This implies a new vision of reality,
one where mutually existing and interrelated communities
create unique and fully self-realized individuals. All of these

ultimately participate in the one great universal community, which in turn participates in the divine community that we call God. We exist as a community in an analogous way to how God exists as the perfect community.

B. Six Conditions for Genuine Human Community

The existence of two levels of reality in human experience raises a question: How can one participate fully at a social level without losing or subsuming one's individuality? Likewise, how can communities create a genuine unity of purpose and a shared life while composed of genuine individuals with distinct minds and life plans? What is the difference between a genuine community and merely natural associations of people directed toward specific ends and purposes, some of which may even be destructive or violent? Royce responds to these challenges through an extensive analysis of community itself.

First Condition: Complex Social Process Over Time. Royce first places community in its proper context. A community, as opposed to a crowd, a mob, or mere association of people, essentially exists as the product of a time process: "A community has a past and will have a future. Its more or less conscious history, real or ideal, is a part of its very essence. A community requires for its existence a history and is greatly aided in its consciousness by a memory."[12] A community not only shares a common mind but also the institutions, organization, traditions, and coherent historical unity that enable it to think and act as a unit over time. This implies the need for a complex and lengthy social process that creates a psychological unity of many selves into one community.[13] This functions fundamentally as a process of individual selves taking on the shared past and expected future of a community in such a way that they can act concurrently and singularly with this community in the present. The individual, then, must be able to extend his/her personal consciousness to take on the vaster and richer consciousness of the community.

Second Condition: Expanded Self-Interpretation —Acquiring New Memory and Hope. Royce believes that this complex social process creates what he calls "communities of memory and hope":

> When many contemporary and distinct individual selves so interpret each his own personal life that each says of an individual past or of a determinate future event or deed: "That belongs to my life," "That occurred or will occur, to me," then these many selves may be defined as hereby constituting, in a perfectly definite and objective, but also a highly significant sense, a community. They may be said to constitute a community *with reference* to that particular past or future event, or group of events, which each of them accepts or interprets as belonging to his own personal past or to his own individual future. A community constituted by the fact that each of its members accepts as part of his own individual life and self the same past events that each of his fellow-members accepts, may be called a *community of memory* . . . [and] *a community of expectation or a community of hope.*[14]

The key to this social process lies in the ability of individuals to interpret their lives in such a way that they can come to understand their own personal lives in terms of a communal life. Individuals can and must extend and enlarge their own lives to include a common past and ideal future that they have not personally experienced or remember. This means that although I did not personally participate in the founding of the community (like the signing of the Declaration of Independence in America) I consider it to be a part of my own personal past (*we* declared independence from England). Similarly, I presume that the future of the whole group is something for which I will take personal responsibility, even though I may not actually live to see this future (giving one's life for one's country so that *we* can be free).

The power to extend one's individual life constitutes the primary condition necessary to form community, its foundation. This power must itself be grounded in a more basic reality:

> This power itself rests upon the principle that, however a man may come by his idea of himself, the self is no mere datum, but is in its essence a life which is interpreted, and which interprets itself, and which, apart from some sort of ideal interpretation, is a mere flight of ideas, or a meaningless flow of feelings, or a vision that sees nothing, or else a barren abstract conception.[15]

Thus, interpretation, and particularly the power of self-interpretation, lies at the heart of the universal social process. The ability to "see" one's life in terms of a greater communal and, finally, cosmological whole, gives individuals the ability to widen and expand their own lives by consciously and freely participating in a community of memory and hope greater than the physical and biological limits that life naturally imposes on us.

Third Condition: Real Communication. In order for the community to function in common ways over time, distinct individuals must be capable of genuine communication and engage in ongoing and progressive communication about their common ideal, past and future events, deeds, persons, etc. This communication should be characterized by intentional and rational forms of conversation in sustained and critical reflection on the common life and goals of the community, and it should include as many members as possible. The whole community must share a common "language" (i.e., a way of communicating with one another on basic values and beliefs), and a method and tradition of communal discourse that has emerged over time and remains both shared and open-ended. In other words, Royce insists that genuine communities must have common forums where both "views of life" and "ways of life" can be discerned and shared.

In Royce's opinon this communication must also be characterized by the literal sharing of lives on the part of all the members of the community. This sharing of lives will primarily be manifested in the sharing of the gifts and talents of each person with the whole community. The community does not become one by a process of melting or blending various selves into a single monolithic self, but by coordinating and orchestrating the lives of many into a single, unified, yet internally diversified, life. Here Royce particularly employs the Pauline metaphor of a body and even compares the community to an orchestra.[16] This sharing of gifts and talents in an orchestrated way creates an inter-dependence between members that enables them to act and work as one body.

This process of real communication is often enabled by one (or somtimes multiple) members acting as "interpreters" for the community. Much like a conductor coordinating an orchestra of communication of gifts, talents, ideas, cultures, and beliefs, the "interpreter" helps the community interpret itself to itself. The interpreter guides the community in a growth in unity while allowing to maintain its diversity and its members' genuine individuality. The interpreter serves the community most fully by helping to build up the individual members and maintaining the dialogue of the whole community over time in a way that enriches all and allows the whole to grow in deeper appreciation of the other and of their common identity.

Fourth Condition: Shared Past Events. Royce believes that the ideally extended past and future selves must have at least some events that are identical for all the selves involved. There must exist some readily identified past events that all members see as part of their own personal history. Royce also assumes that these past events must be recalled, nurtured, and sustained by the whole community through common commemorative acts and ritual events.[17] For Americans, the signing of the

Declaration of Independence serves as such a shared past event. All Americans, regardless of when they actually immigrated to the United States, annually remember the event, celebrate it, and assume some direct connection and identity with this founding event. For the Jewish people, the Exodus event and the Passover celebration function in this way. It is a past event that is common to all Jews regardless of their other religious and cultural differences. For Christians, the Paschal Mystery (Jesus' death and resurrection), and the sacraments of Christian initiation (baptism, confirmation, and eucharist) that commemorate this event, assume this foundational role. Christian identity revolves around this central organizing event and its manifold implications that unites even those Christians otherwise divided by historical and doctrinal conflicts.

Fifth Condition: Voluntary Cooperation. In the power of self-interpretation and the principles which underlie it Royce believed he had found the key to his ongoing attempt to solve the problem of the "one and the many." In his mature theory of community he discerned the possibility of portraying a genuine unity of consciousness that still allowed for, and even necessitated, a variety of individual members. This schema bases a shared unity of life on the conscious cooperation of many individuals. This only comes about through the free choice of self-interpretation of the individual. Genuine community, therefore, cannot be coerced or imposed. Cooperation must be chosen and developed over time, and must become for the individuals involved a kind "conscious art."[18] For Royce, this implies that the many kinds of social groups that we are born into or immersed through historical events—religions, national identities, political parties, regional or language based social structures, economic class—can only become genuine communities if the mature members consciously, critically, and freely ratify their affiliation with and make a commitment to the life of the collective group. Passive acquiescence or minimal participation by a majority of the membership tends to signal a lack of the type of real cooperation necessary for the genuine community to exist in the way that Royce envisions.

Sixth Condition: Love as Loyalty to Loyalty. What enables this form of conscious cooperation and develops the individual characteristics and habits upon which it is based? Clearly society itself does not necessarily foster either reality. Royce believes that the answer lies exclusively in a love that empowers the kind of conscious cooperation necessary for true community:

> Love furnishes that basis for the consciousness of the community which intelligence, without love, in a highly complex social realm can no longer furnish. Such love—such loyalty—depends not upon losing sight of the variety of the callings of individuals, but upon seeing in the successful cooperation of all members precisely that event which the individual member most eagerly loves as his own fulfillment.[19]

Love creates a type of vision or insight that enables one to remain loyal to a conscious unity and to a life that we cannot in fact see at any one time. For Royce, love itself exists as a kind of interpretation of reality that in turn empowers the self-interpretation required to build up the conscious unity and cooperation that moves us to a realm higher than ourselves. Love ultimately grounds the self-interpretation and implies a power that is grounded in a view or vision of reality that is beyond our individual scope. "Love, when it comes, comes as from above" according to Royce, which implies that the ultimate source of community lies in the intervening and creative power of love (love here not just meaning an emotion but a type of knowledge, an insight or interpretation, and the efficacious power to transform the self in the light of this knowledge). This source of love transcends both the individual and social levels of reality, although it works through both, and must finally be seen as divine.[20]

C. Community and the Ideology of Individualism

Over against individualistic constructs of natural existence, Royce's formulation of human experience offers a clear account of reality as made of two irreducible elements: individuals and communities. For Royce, "modern" understandings of community as a mere voluntary aggregate of otherwise separate and "independent" individuals, not only falsely misrepresents the nature of community, but misapprehends the very nature of reality itself. Mistaking individual subjective experience as the sole foundation of all reality, modern and post-modern thought have unwittingly created an ideology of individualism that has increasingly diminished the ability of many human beings to achieve genuine autonomy and individuality. This false and misleading emphasis on individualistic constructs of experience has been especially devastating when applied to the religious dimensions of human experience. Without the essential social and communal dimension of religious experience a person cannot fully recognize or respond to the offer of divine grace that such an experience represents. Central to the desire for, and reliance on, religious insight is the development and the practice of a rich and fruitful communal faith tradition.

Royce convincingly shows that a community depends on a time process, the ability of individual persons to expand their personal identities to take on that of a community, and the necessity of a community for the individual to ever attain autonomy and maturity. Likewise, by defining the world as composed of an interlocking system of communities, Royce demonstrates the profound communal nature of creation itself. He also shows how the fullness of any individual human life can only be achieved in a communal context, as the fullness of any reality depends upon its relationship to the rest of reality through communion.

The Three Essential Charisms that Create and Sustain Community

"Become imitators of me, as I am an imitator of Christ" (1 Cor 11:1). The Apostle Paul reminded the early Church at Corinth that no one can be a Christian without participating in a community of people who mutually mediate Christ's presence to one another. Likewise, he insists that no community can truly manifest the risen Christ without individual members who model and express new life and new possibilities to the community. For human beings, all learning is based on imitation. We adapt and assimilate our thought patterns and behavior in reference to those that we observe around us.

A community requires for its existence animating and empowering individuals who make this shared life possible. I have already mentioned the essential role played by the interpreter/guide in the community life. This charism is necessary not only for the growth and development of a community but for maintaining its unity over time (as explained earlier). In addition, there seem to be three critical elements or charisms necessary to create, maintain, and redeem genuine community. These charisms can arise from different individuals working in unison or, sometimes, from a single individual embodying all of these. Each person in the community can and must cultivate these elements or charisms to some degree. They are: preachers/poets/storytellers, teachers/servants, and martyrs/prophets.

Preachers/poets/storytellers. Every community must be able to imagine itself, and it must be "imaginable" to each of its members. There is a critical need for members to create and articulate the shared unconscious and pre-rational consciousness of the community. There must be some members of the community who can tell the shared memories of the group and help others to envision the future. These are the charisms that help the members of the community to see and hear and feel differently, to have a sense of history and purpose, and enable the community to act out of hope rather than fear.

Teachers/servants: models of genuine loyalty. We model life to one another through our concrete daily actions. We enable loyalty, fidelity, and commitment in other people by our own example. Every community must have people willing to live faithfully and intentionally so as to enable other people's faithfulness. We learn through imitation, and so learn to live genuinely through the example of others. The community needs individuals who are fully dedicated to the community and its shared life in a way that is manifest, visible and imitable.

Martyrs/prophets: models of atoning love. For any community to survive it must have members that have the heroic willingness to suffer in order to bring forth new life. There will always be a need to heal and reconcile the community, and there is *always* a degree of disloyalty and betrayal in any community. There must be, therefore, counterbalancing and transforming deeds of reconciliation and love to re-create a broken community. Every community needs people with a ready and utter willingness to give up their own life, their own needs and desires, for the good of the whole. This is not to be confused with what has become popularly known as "co-dependence." Co-dependence is an unhealthy and selfish dependence of one person on the sicknesses and brokenness of another. Genuine atoning love is never self-righteous, nor is it the fruit of self-hatred, intimidation, or false humility. Atoning love is ultimately rooted in the faith that our actions can be redemptive, and that atoning deeds have a mysterious power to bring about transformation in ourselves and others.

We all know people who have these charisms to some degree. We have all lived with people who "modeled" community for us. In the Christian community these three elements are most clearly seen in Jesus Christ.

Jesus gives us the idea or image of the community and its constituting story: the kingdom of God. Through the example of his life and ministry, he teaches us what this vision practically entails. He shows us how to live, and thereby enables others to live in this kingdom. He finally gives his life for this vision, atoning for the betrayal of it—not in anger but deeply trusting in the reality and transforming power of God's reign. Jesus' atoning love brings new life by re-gathering and reconciling the community and enabling it to fully be what it was meant to be.

Christian communities are to be genuine in that they imitate Jesus Christ. They preach community and witness to it through their lives and their atoning, self-sacrificing love. To follow Christ means to be filled with the Spirit, to become part of genuine community that acts as a *sign* to the wider society of the meaning and purpose of the world.

Constituting the Christian Community

1. What Makes a Community Christian?

The Christian community locates its hermeneutical key in the life, death, and resurrection of Jesus Christ. He constitutes the new community by serving it as a preacher, teacher, servant, prophet, and source of the Spirit. The coordinator of the community is the Spirit of Christ, who connects the individual with the community, and the community with other communities, to form the body of the risen Christ.

2. "The People of God" as the Metaphor for the Christian Community

This leads me back to chapter 2 of *Lumen Gentium* and to assert that "The People of God" serves as the best metaphor for the Church of Christ. In my opinion, this metaphor best explains the historical scope of God's plan of salvation as it encompasses both the "old" and "new" covenants, and the visible and invisible community of believers. The image of "The People of God" forces us to invoke our imagination to picture a community that includes people of all times and places, races and cultures, united together in the one saving plan of God. This vision serves as the foundation for all other reflections on that specific part of the people of God we call the Christian Church.

3. How is the Christian Church also a Community?

The term "Church" denotes a particular type of community. "Christian Church" describes a community that self-consciously lives in memory of Jesus Christ and in the hope of his coming again in the glory of the kingdom of God. This community, begun by the Spirit of the risen Christ, lives, grows, and develops during the historical time between the Paschal Event and the *parousia* (Greek for the Second Coming of Christ). It exists as a sign and expression of both events. The memory and hope of this community are preserved in the Gospel and proclaimed constantly to both those "within" and "outside" of it. Evangelization through the proclamation of the Gospel in word and deed functions as the primary mission of this community.

An intricate web of communications characterizes the Christian community. This identity of life lives through both the community's shared tradition of interpretation, as well as through the "communion of charisms" that literally creates and enlivens each community of believers. This tradition constitutes each church as an ongoing community of interpretation that not only transmits its past memory but also continually interprets that very tradition in terms of the present context and signs of the times. The specific expectation of the coming of the reign of God proclaimed by Jesus Christ informs this community of interpretation and guides it in its ongoing deliberations and dialogue.

No real shared identity of life and actions would be possible without the conscious participation of every member in the actual life of the community. The Christian Church, prompted and guided by the Spirit of Christ, must continually call forth, share, and mutually depend on the gifts of each member. This sharing of charisms distinguishes the Church from other communities. While many of the charisms needed in a church will be the same as those that are needed in any genuine community, the church requires that special charisms be appropriated and shared. These charisms (particularly the gifts of prayer, discernment of spirits, mediation of God's presence through ritual and preaching, the service of caring for one another and for those outside of the community) constitute the direct patrimony of Jesus to the Church.

All members of the Church share directly in the once-and-for-all saving event of the Paschal Mystery through the sacraments of initiation. As Christians we believe that we literally "put on Christ," entering into his life, death, and resurrection through baptism, confirmation, and the eucharist. Through the remembering (*anamnesis*) of Jesus' atoning act of love in the eucharist, each Christian and each community literally shares in the saving life, death, and resurrection of Christ. These sacraments of initiation serve not only as the first step of our life in community but as the ongoing event of God's salvific offer in human history. While not every Christian community interprets these sacraments of initiation in the same way, they remain central to the long tradition of the whole Church of Christ.

Defining the Church of Christ as a Community of Communities

The Church of Christ can be characterized as accepting the same basic creed: an interpretation of the triune life of God and of God's plan for the universe. This creedal formula offers the most basic and traditional interpretation of God and God's relationship to the world through creation and the missions of the Son and the Spirit in human history. The Church itself, as the visible manifestation of these missions, also serves as the object of belief and as the expression of the more basic belief in God's communal and corporate plan of salvation for the whole cosmos.

1. The Church of Christ and the Roman Catholic Church

Given these generalizations, we can define the Church of Christ as all the visible communities that share in this single identity of life. This community exists then as a community of communities, in which each of the individual and particular churches participate. The Church of Christ lives in (subsists) the Roman Catholic Church in a vital and important way. This means that without the Roman Catholic Church the Church of Christ could not exist as a genuine community of communities; she would be unfulfilled and deficient in a substantial and essential way. Likewise, because the Roman Catholic Church lives in the Church of Christ, she lives and shares in the wider community of the whole Body of Christ analogously to how an individual belongs to a community. The Roman Catholic Church achieves the fullness of her own unique identity and purpose within this larger community of memory and hope, which is the invisible Church of Christ. The Church must fully enter into the web of communications characteristic of this larger community, and offer to contribute her charisms as well as receive those of other communities. The visible boundaries of the Roman Catholic Church do not exhaust the Church of Christ. Nor does the Church have a monopoly on the presence of the Spirit. Even the Church of Christ exists as a community within wider spheres of community (the community of all the people of faith, the universal human community, the universe itself, and the divine community). No church or community, no matter how large or how old or how complex, can exist outside and apart from ever-wider spheres of community. Interrelationship and mutual dependence between communities, all participating in a wider process of cosmic unification, constitute the very nature of any single community and of community itself.

2. The Roman Catholic Church is also a Community of Communities

The Roman Catholic Church must be similarly understood as a community of communities or a Church of churches. This interpretation represents the oldest tradition of the Church, and it conforms to the nature of the Church as a community. Following the pattern outlined by Royce, we can envision the Roman Catholic Church as a community composed of smaller communities, themselves composed of communities of authentic individuals. This context clarifies the relationship between the universal Church and particular churches, a relationship that simply exists as a variation on the fundamental relationship between the universal and particular. To this relationship applies Royce's insistence on two fundamental and irreducible levels of existence—individual and community. Both levels serve as necessary components of the one reality—neither can be reduced or derived from the other. In this sense, then, the universal Church exists in and "is formed out of" the local churches, while not simply functioning as the sum of these many diverse parts. The universal community has its own identity of life and recognizable shared activity that each of the local churches participates in, even though they do not monopolize or control it in a direct way. On the other hand, the universal Church cannot ever be considered ontologically or temporally prior to the local Churches, nor can it absorb or meld them in a way that detracts from their genuine autonomy. Both the individual, local church and the universal Roman Catholic Church need one another for their existence, and both must participate together in ever-wider circles of community as well. In this sense, it is not a matter of "higher" and "lower" forms of Church existence and authority. Both the universal and the particular each exist as fully complete and inter-dependent.

3. The Local Church in the Roman Catholic Church

The Roman Catholic Church tends to define the local church as a diocese or as a particular church with its own unique history and identity that nevertheless understands itself to be in union with the universal Roman Catholic Church. Within the diocese the same communitarian principle would apply as previously articulated. Each particular church would itself be composed of smaller and diverse communities with different purposes, histories, and functions. The basic level of community grounding the ever-widening circles of community in the Roman Catholic Church are those "altar communities" where the eucharist can be celebrated, and the basic community of memory and hope can flourish at a genuinely personal and mutually interdependent level. All Catholic Christians are incorporated into this basic level of community through their baptism and have a right to expect both the eucharist and the authentic sharing of life and gifts that it represents. Inasmuch as Christians are not helped to access this level of community, either because of members' selfishness and lack of conversion or because of institutional rigidity and intransigence to the promptings of the Spirit, the community fails to be fully authentic and significant. The bishop of the diocese is responsible to see that the conditions for the possibility of genuine ecclesial life are present at this level of community.

4. The Role and Function of the Bishop in the Roman Catholic Church

The bishop functions in the diocese in an analogous way to the "interpreter" in Royce's conception of the community of interpretation. The interpreter serves the community by orchestrating the sharing of the charisms, directing the overall life of the local community for each member to grow and flourish. Moreover, the interpreter serves to coordinate, but never monopolize, the process of interpretation of the Tradition and the discernment of the will of the Spirit within each diocese. Similarly, Vatican II insists that all the bishops act collegially to coordinate this process at a universal level. While there is the ongoing development of the collegial under-standing of the bishop's role at the level of the universal Church, we must also ask ourselves how this collegiality is to be extended into each diocese. The whole community of faithful shares in different but important ways in the collegial process of interpreting God's will and acting on the basis of this shared interpretation. Similarly, each part of the Church must obediently listen and respond to the will of the Spirit. This is precisely where a positive and strongly developed understanding of the discernment of the charisms will be critically important. While by his office the bishop will have certain specific charisms, one of the primary ones is to coordinate and facilitate the many other charisms essential to the life of the community. By virtue of his very charism, the bishop cannot exercise his office in isolation or in contradiction to the profound interplay of many other charisms. This implies that participative forms of decision-making and shared responsibility and accountability at every level must function as a foundational and organizational principle for the internal governing of the Church.

5. The Community (College) of Bishops as a Community of Service

Bishops in communion function as a community with a very special and unique charism within the wider community of the Church. This community, called the hierarchy, was charged by Christ with guiding the Church in continuing his own vision and mission of working for the reign of God (LG 18–28). The bishops are intended by Christ to serve as a permanent and visible sign of unity and of the Tradition, grown over centuries, that the faith has been passed on from one generation to another under the guidance of the Holy Spirit. This unique community, in union with the Bishop of Rome, serves to guide the Roman Catholic Church as interpreters and teachers, maintaining over time and distance the unity of the many diverse churches that characterize the real life of the Church. They maintain the complex social processes of the community and the continuity of the memory and hope of the wider community. Thus, whatever differences may define individuals and communities within the Church, they will be able to hold some basic dimensions of life in common.

This community also helps the wider community to grow and develop over time by thoughtful and careful deliberation on changes and adaptations that must be made for the good of the whole.

6. The Unique Role of the Bishop of Rome

Given Royce's schema, I believe that we can interpret the Bishop of Rome as similarly functioning as the interpreter of the community on a universal level. The universal interpreter must be concerned foremost with mediating the unity of the whole group rather than acting on his own behalf or protecting the interest of some parts of the community. This unique charism can serve a critical function in bringing about the much needed unity of all churches in the one Church of Christ. He can also risk to obstruct and impede the universal process if he does not genuinely act as the willing and obedient servant of the divine interpreter Spirit. For this reason, while the universal interpreter will always arise out of a specific community, he must willingly put the universal community of communities above these origins and work for an end much higher than the preservation or advancement of any single community. Ultimately, the Bishop of Rome, however, following in the footsteps of the Apostles Peter and Paul, has been commissioned to unite the whole Church as a single sign and witness to the world of the saving power of Jesus Christ. In his role as the interpreter guide of the community of communities—the Church of the churches—the Bishop of Rome strives to fulfill the final prayer of Jesus, "May they all be one" (Jn 17:20–21).

Part III: Sacrament and Sacramentality
The Church as a Sign of the Reign of God

If the Trinity, specifically the "rediscovery" of the centrality of the Holy Spirit, was the most important new theological insight to ground the constitutions and documents of Vatican II, then the vast expanse in understanding and meaning of "sacrament," and its pervasive and central presence throughout the texts, is an equally important development to emerge from the Council. In common knowledge and in much of theology in general before the Council, the term "sacrament" referred to the seven sacraments of the Church. The common usage of the term, however, actually derives from a much broader and richer connotation, and "sacrament" in its fullest sense actually held the key to understanding the nature and mission of the Church. As I have stated earlier, "sacrament" and "sacramentality" serve as organizing concepts around which the Church articulated its relationship with both Jesus Christ and the world, and then understood its mission in the world and to the world.

Within a Christian world view, sacrament has a very unique meaning. It connotes a powerful sign or symbol of God's presence in the world that actually makes this power and presence real or "more real." Sacraments, however, are not magic. Sacraments "work" in a special way, but in a way consistent with and related to the way the whole world operates. Signs and symbols are part of everyday life, and they affect the actions and behavior of every person. Scientific and other kinds of philosophical or cultural world views all depend on signs and symbols to function and "work" as well. Given the centrality of sacrament, sacraments, and sacramentality, we need to understand how a "sacramental" world view fits in with other ways of looking at the world, and with how the world "works" in general.

Symbolic Structure of All Reality

The two preceding parts of this chapter have presumed that there exists a symbolic structure to all of reality. The Holy Spirit forms people into genuine communities of interpretation and guides them in correctly "reading" the signs of the times. Thus they may live out the plan of God for the world and help bring about the full unity of the community of communities in the very life of the triune God. Both pneumatology and community presuppose that reality is profoundly interconnected and interrelated. While these connections and relationships are real and immediate, they must in some way be mediated, for us to experience them as separate or distinct. This is what happens through signs. Signs both connect and distinguish things from one another; they help us to know that other things exist and yet also require us to interpret their meaning and purpose.

Human beings live in one vast "sign system." We are constantly sending and receiving, interpreting and being interpreted, through signs. We interpret signs through other signs, which are in turn the source of further interpretation. This is how knowledge, whether scientific, economic, social, political, personal, or religious, is gained in this world. Everything —from reading the paper to knowing when a baby needs to be fed, from driving to work to answering the phone, from finding a cure for a disease to falling in love—requires adequately interpreting signs. Every person, no matter how young or old, each day interprets many of the thousands of signs received in terms of the practical decisions that determine the activities, feelings, thoughts, and reactions that make up daily life. Unique to each person is the adequacy and validity with which they interpret the signs that they chose to interpret or that present themselves that day.

Obviously, given the enormous number of signs that make up our daily lives, it is impossible for any individual to completely master interpreting more than a small portion of them. The best way to interpret signs is by belonging to a community of people who want to consciously grow at interpreting similar types of signs as ourselves. Communities of interpretation will determine which signs we interpret and how we interpret them. It is this process of interpretation that shapes our individual lives: our character, habits, personality traits, skills, interests, talents, etc. Over the course of our lives we will belong to many different communities of interpretation, to some consciously, to others unconsciously. Examples are our family, schools, churches, local civic communities, states, governments, cultures, economic systems, careers, teams, clubs, social movements, etc. The goal of a truly mature adult life is to freely choose the best community of interpretation for us and to participate fully in it by organizing our life around it and its shared understanding of the significance of the world. To be fully and consciously faithful to an authentic community of interpretation that believes that the world has true meaning is the highest level of human experience and individual autonomy, an extremely decisive and important interpretation of our own individual life.

Types of Signs

Given the centrality of signs to human knowing and life in general, there has been a growing interest in the theory of signs (called *semiotics*), and the field of study has grown extensively. Nevertheless, the American founder of this field, Charles Sanders Peirce (a contemporary and friend of Josiah Royce),[21] while developing a complex system of signs, offered three basic types of signs upon which he based others. While these three types of signs can be combined in various arrangements and altered in multiple ways to create numerous other types of signs, they remain fundamentally helpful to thinking about the meaning of sacrament in a sign structured reality.[22] A basic explanation follows:

1. *Icons*. Here the sign resembles that which it signifies, but the relationship is not completely direct and concrete.[23] A portrait of a young woman acts as a sign of what she looks like. For Peirce, a diagram of a house, a painting of a garden, a statue of a man on a horse are all types of icons. All of these require that the sign be acknowledged and accepted as a genuine resemblance by the receiver. They look like or sound like or feel like what they are meant to convey to the receiver. An icon can even portray something that does not really exist, like a gargoyle or a unicorn, if the receiver knows what they are "supposed" to look like and can acknowledge it in this sign.

2. *Index*. Here the sign directly conveys what it signifies: the relationship is direct, concrete and causal. Examples include a finger pointing to an object, a door knock declaring someone's

presence on the other side, a car horn warning of an approaching vehicle, a weathervane showing the direction and intensity of the wind, and smoke arising directly from a fire. The receiver can choose to interpret it or not—but the event or sign itself exists regardless of whether the receiver acknowledges and interprets it.

3. *Symbol.* Here the relationship between the sign and the receiver is completely arbitrary and requires the active cooperation of the receiver to be received and interpreted. The receiver has to make the connection between two (at least) things that are not necessarily (like an index) or even similarly (like an icon) connected or related. The most pervasive and fundamental kind of symbol is language. Words have meaning only when the receiver can interpret them correctly. Language is the sign-system that unites human minds and upon which every human being depends for survival. At the same time we depend on the active cooperation of individuals to function at all. All complex forms of signification (stories, arguments, education, rituals, customs, socio-political-economic systems) build on symbolic forms of signs. Symbols, therefore, are the major and most systematic manifestation of signs that we experience in daily life. Likewise, language serves as the most ordinary and common form of a symbol, which grounds most forms of human interaction and human thought itself.

Different kinds of signs can interact in different ways, and therefore the same object can also be signified in different ways. For instance, my finger can point to a bird and so my finger is an *index* of the bird. A painting of a bird constitutes an *icon* of the bird. The term "bird" itself, however, acts as a *symbol* of the bird, because there is no direct connection between the bird, the speaker, and the interpretant without the structure of language that allows the relationship to exist. It is important to note here that signs are not mutually exclusive but interact in different ways to convey different modes of relationships within the vast sign system that makes up our world. Obviously, these very primary modes of relationship grow more complex as the analysis of the sign system deepens and expands. For our purposes, however, these three basic types of signs are sufficient to explain the unique type of sign that we call a sacrament.

A sacrament is a unique type of sign that functions simultaneously at all three modes of signification/relationship. The most common definition of sacrament is an "efficacious sign of grace"[24] or a "sign that makes real what it signifies."[25] This conforms well to how a complex sign that is at once an icon, index, and symbol would function. Our belief is that a sacrament is a type of sign that does more than simply represent a reality; it also profoundly mediates or conveys that reality. It portrays a saving event in history, by God through Christ in the power of the Holy Spirit. It also offers that same saving power literally, in the present, through the sign itself, by the power of the sacramental event that is mediated by the Church through the Word. In other words, a sacrament is an *icon*/portrayal of a past event, which is a direct *index* of God's present action, which is expressed and manifested to the participants through *symbols*: particularly, but not limited to, language. For instance, a sacrament of the Church, like eucharist, portrays or remembers (*anamnesis* is the special Greek word that means to remember or recall in this triadic way) the Last Supper of Christ and the gift of his own life for us in his passion, death and resurrection (the Paschal Mystery). It points directly and concretely to this saving event in the present in the lives of those who participate in the liturgical remembrance, and it is enacted through a variety of symbols: readings, prayers, preaching, music, ritual actions, symbolic objects, etc. Although it might be possible to only observe or describe the sacramental event in terms of one type of sign, the fullness of the sacrament resides in the profound interaction of all three types. It is through this full interaction that the sign makes real what it signifies and is an efficacious and powerful instrument of God's grace.

Sacraments shape and form Christian communities. They are the source of our individual and common interpretation of the world, our unifying memory and hope, what empowers our voluntary cooperation and communication, and enables the self-sacrificing love that makes genuine community possible. The sacraments are intentional, creative, and communal signs that resemble, point to, and interpret a reality greater than ourselves—the reality to which we have given our lives, the reign of God. But more than just having sacraments at the center of our lives as Christian communities, we believe that each Christian community is *meant to be a sacrament*. The profound insight and great recovery of Vatican II were not just the centrality of the sacraments for the lives of Christians but the deeper realization that the Church itself was called to be a sacrament for the wider community of the world to which it belonged. This broader dimension of sacramentality lies at the heart of what we are calling communion ecclesiology.

The Chain of Sacramentality and the Catholic World View

The documents of Vatican II recovered the ancient understanding of sacrament as referring primarily to the Latin word *sacramentum*, which itself was the translation of the Greek term *mysterion*.[26] In scripture, m*ysterion* refers to the visible manifestation of God's saving presence and action. This salvific presence, usually invisible and available only through the eyes of faith, was occasionally made visible and concrete in some unique revelation that expressed and clarified God's plan in a vivid way. This type of dynamic and concrete revelation of God's invisible and pervasive presence was most dramatically and ultimately revealed in the person of Jesus Christ. Jesus Christ as the "Word made flesh" who lived among us (Jn 1:14) most clearly serves as the primal *mysterion*, the most basic and fundamental sacrament of God.

Paul refers to Jesus Christ as follows:

> He is the image of the invisible God, the firstborn of all creation; for in him all things in heaven and on earth were created, things visible and invisible. . . . He himself is before all things, and in him all things hold

together. He is the head of the body, the Church; he is the beginning, the firstborn from the dead, so that he might come to have first place in everything. For in him all the fullness of God pleased to dwell, and through him God was pleased to reconcile to himself all things . . . provided that you continue to persevere steadfast in faith, without drifting from the hope promised by the gospel that you heard which has proclaimed to every creature under heaven. (Col 1:15–23)

Jesus Christ is the most fundamental form of sacramental sign as we have come to understand it. Jesus Christ is an *icon,* an image, of the one invisible God; through his life and actions humans can see what God is like and what God intended for human earthly existence to be like from before creation itself. Jesus Christ is an *index* of God; the fullness of God literally lives in him and is reconciling "all things" to God's own self. And finally, Jesus Christ serves as the most basic *symbol* of God; he came to proclaim and explain the good news of God's plan of salvation, called the reign of God. Through his life and actions he offered hope and promise to people, not only in his own time but throughout history, by forming a community that would have his Spirit and would continue to spread the good news. Jesus Christ, therefore, is the *sacrament*, that unique and special type of sign upon which all of the other forms of sacraments derive. Jesus Christ is God's self-communication in history in a powerful and ultimate mode. In the vast array of signs that make up our world, Jesus Christ stands as the most important one in that he gives direction, meaning, and value to all the other signs that shape our world.

The Church as the Body of Christ—a living community filled with his divine Spirit—also "is in the nature of a sacrament" (LG 1). The Church acts as a vibrant and life-giving sign of Jesus Christ's ongoing presence and offer of salvation to the world. In an analogous manner to the way that Jesus is a sacrament of God, the Church serves as a sacrament of Jesus Christ.

We see this clearly in numerous places in the New Testament, but most strongly in the writings of Paul. The community, re-formed after the resurrection and filled with Christ's own *pneuma*/Spirit, is meant to serve as an icon of Jesus Christ by reminding the world, through its own life and actions, of Jesus' life and actions (Acts 2:42–47; 4:34–37; Rom 12:1–21; 1 Cor 12:1–31). Paul says of the Christian community:

> So if anyone is in Christ, there is a new creation: everything old has passed away; see, everything has become new! All of this is from God, who reconciled himself to us through Christ, and has given us his ministry of reconciliation; that is, in Christ God was reconciling the world to himself, not counting their trespasses against them, and entrusting the message of reconciliation to us. *So we are ambassadors for Christ, since God is making his appeal through us*; we entreat you be reconciled to God. (2 Cor 17–20)

The sacramental pattern that emerges in the Church is literally an *icon* of Christ, having been made new through his redeeming action. As ambassadors, the Christian communities are also *indices,* because God is working directly through them to continue his work of reconciliation. Moreover, the Churches act as ongoing *symbols* of Christ, because they are ambassadors entrusted with both the task of reconciliation and the ministry, for the transmission of the story and the message of Jesus Christ. For Paul the Church is clearly meant to serve as an efficacious sign of Jesus Christ to the world through her life (actions and service) and her proclamation (both in word and deed). This is her fundamental mission and purpose.

Sacrament and the Seven Sacraments

Vatican II reappropriated this primary understanding of the Church, which emerged from the Council as the central interpretation of the whole event. As a sacrament of Jesus Christ, the Church organizes itself in a way that helps it to best serve and carry out this most basic and fundamental reason for her existence. All the dimensions of the Church's "inner" life—the hierarchy, other ministries, the sacraments, governmental structures, etc.—serve the building up of the Church's sacramental character and mission. Similarly, all of the Church's "external" actions—like services by the local or universal Church on behalf of other people, particularly people in need—directly reflect the sacramental character of the Church whose only goal is to imitate and re-present Christ to the modern world.

The traditional seven sacraments of the Church—baptism, confirmation, eucharist, reconciliation, marriage, holy orders, and anointing of the sick—serve to create and build up the community and to hold the community of communities together in unity until the day when Christ comes again. Each individual sacrament is itself an *icon*, *index,* and *symbol*, rooted in, dependent on, and derived from the one sacrament—Jesus Christ and his efficacious and continuing presence in the Church.[27] Each sacrament uniquely represents (*iconically*) either some part of Christ's own life and ministry or God's plan for the Church and the world. These special signs are empowered with Christ's own *pneuma* so that they truly effect (*index*) and bring about what they promise and proclaim. And finally, these sacraments are not magic but are enmeshed in an entire *symbolic structure*. This structure both explains and deepens the meaning of the event through the use of concrete and ordinary symbols, rituals, scripture, stories, prayers, hymns and other forms of evocative and intuitive expressions, which interpret the wider meaning of the sacramental event for the lives of all the participants.

As explained earlier, these sacraments serve multiple functions. They form and shape the ongoing conversion and life of faith of the individual and community, literally building up the community and orientating it toward its mission of representing Christ to the world; they unite each individual with the community and each local community with the wider universal community; they reveal dramatically and visibly the power of the Holy Spirit at work in each human life and the whole community; and they each point to and help to bring about the second coming of Christ when the reign of God will finally be established for all eternity. This implies that the sacraments are profoundly "weighted" signs—they mean much more than they can ever fully express. In this sense, they help us to understand that all sacramental signs can never be fully and completely interpreted in this life.

Sacraments and the Church as a Community of Interpretation

Sacraments are signs that cannot be fully seen or known even by an extremely large or old community of interpretation. Sacraments, as signs of God's own self-communication, are by their nature inexhaustible in their interpretation. This means that although we can know a great deal about Christ and the Church and the sacraments, etc., we can never have the final word or the final interpretation of the rich and profound meaning of these infinitely meaningful signs. The process of interpretation must be ongoing and emerging because of the very depth and power of signification that these unique types of signs offer. The Church's authority to interpret them (including its own self-interpretation) derives precisely from its own sacramentality: from the fact that it is an efficacious sign of the reign of God in Jesus Christ. But it would lose its authority if it chose to stop listening and interpreting the ongoing revelation that the sacrament of Jesus Christ offers to the world. The Church is most true to its own authentic interpreting authority when it serves the world as an ongoing, dialogical, and listening servant to both the sacrament of Jesus Christ and the "signs of the times."

The Special Sacramentality of the Word in the Catholic Tradition

Among the many brilliant and splendid recoveries made by the Second Vatican Council, the centrality of the Word of God in all liturgical rites and in the life of the Church as a whole remains particularly gratifying.[28] In the very first Constitution, *Sacrosanctum Concilium*, the Church returned to the ancient principle that there could be no liturgical rites, and hence no sacraments, without the Word as part of them.[29] Sacred scripture and preaching about it manifest the very presence of God and express the Word made flesh: Jesus Christ himself. The Constitution states that Christ is really "present in His word, since it is He Himself who speaks when the holy Scriptures are read in the church" (SC, 7).

Sacred scripture by itself, apart from its active proclamation in a community, is a living *symbol* of God's saving power in history. Actively expressed and proclaimed in a community of faith, this *symbol* can also become an *icon* by literally enlivening the Body of Christ; it can serve as an *index,* because it is Christ's own Spirit that enables and is conveyed by the hearing and seeing and feeling of the presence of Christ through the various forms of proclaiming the Word. This does not mean that the Word is an eighth sacrament alongside the other seven. Nor does it mean that the Word is a kind of proto-sacrament that necessarily precedes or forms the others. Rather, it implies that the Word, as the fundamental symbol system of the Judeo-Christian tradition, grounds and participates in every sacrament, and binds together and unites along with the Holy Spirit the "chain of sacramentality" that links the whole created order. The Word is sacramental in that it can both come alive in the midst of and enliven the rich possibilities of God's manifold presence in the world through the gathering of a community of believers and the power of the Holy Spirit, so that "wherever two or three are gathered in my name I am there" (Mt 18:20).

The Church as a Genuine *Icon* of Christ

Through God's generous offer and promise of grace, the Church always maintains its capability to serve as an *index* of the Holy Spirit. Similarly, the great Tradition of the Church, beginning with sacred scripture itself, holds and sustains the *symbolic* dimension of the life of the Church. In this sense, the Church is always assured that these two dimensions of its sacramentality will remain as secure and constant foundations and resources for the life of the Church. The efficacy of the Church as a sacramental sign, then, rests with its ability to portray, represent, and serve as an *icon* of Christ to the world. How effectively the Church represents Christ depends upon the free choice of its members to live as Christ lived and to treat others as he would treat them. The Church's sacramental efficacy depends upon its ability to look like Christ to those within and especially outside of it. Will people ever automatically or reflexively recognize the Church as the Body of Christ? That is the fundamental question that faces the Church today.

For the Church to be fully a sacrament it must do more than claim to be an *icon* of Christ; it must literally witness to the reign of God through its shared, concrete, and daily life. The Church's role as signifying the risen Christ and his offer, hope, and promise of an eternal shared life with the triune God, obviously cannot be separated from the function its communities play in announcing, "witnessing to," and actually participating in this reality. The Church as a sacrament (as a sign and initial participation, through the efficacious action of the Spirit, in God's plan for the universe) represents the meaning of communion at its deepest level. This communion, however, is only possible if the Church literally and authentically embodies the virtues and values that she proclaims in Christ's name.

If Royce is correct and the universe reveals itself to be an ongoing and emerging process of interpretation, then the role of any sign within this process cannot be overestimated. If the Church intends to function in this process as a sign of God's own interpretation of this reality, then the moral and ethical responsibility required of the Church seems overwhelming. That the Church functions as this type of sign, not through its own power but through the mysterious and utterly gratuitous power of God acting through both Jesus and the Spirit, mitigates the inadequacy of human beings in this process. Nevertheless, Jesus makes it quite clear that while salvation ultimately comes from God, God has chosen humans to cooperate with the divine life in achieving this goal. The significance of the Church's sacramentality, therefore, does depend to some extent on the ethical and moral life of the Church's members and of the community as a whole.

The internal life of the Church must reflect and authenticate the message which it preaches to the rest of the world. Any violation of human rights within the Church (such as clericalism, monopolization and obstruction of the charisms, and the use of power to manipulate and coerce other human beings) threatens to damage, perhaps irrevocably, her sacramental power.[30]

Similarly, I believe that all of the Christian Churches need to engage in ecumenism. The Church cannot serve as a visible and efficacious sign of the possibility of the unity of all creation if the communities that compose her cannot achieve basic levels of unity and harmony among themselves. The visible disunity of the Churches violates the most basic premise and proclamation of Christianity. This situation compels all the Churches through mutual dialogue and self-sacrificing acts of atoning love to begin a serious process of reconciliation and reunification. This means that every community, including the Roman Catholic Church, must begin to rethink and revise itself differently and in new modes of existence in mutual cooperation with the other Christian communities. The Bishop of Rome has a special responsibility and obligation to facilitate and coordinate this process.[31]

The Second Vatican Council, and subsequently many Christians, strongly espoused the belief that the Church's sacramental efficacy exists as intimately tied to her literal solidarity with and treatment of the poor, the outcast, and the powerless. If the Church truly represents the plan of God in imitation of Jesus Christ, then she must find her true home among the poor, suffering, and sinful people of this world as he did. The practical test of the Church's sacramentality is her willingness to share her resources and material goods with all people in need. This obligation does not necessarily fall first of all to the universal community, but its most valuable significance will come when it can be witnessed at the most daily and ordinary levels of Christian communal life.

The concrete criteria for judging the genuine sacramentality of the Church resides in the level and quality of the *metanoia* she enables in her members, in her communal life, and in the wider community in which she lives. For the Church to act as an authentic sign of the possibilities of graced transformation and ongoing conversion for all human beings, she must literally exhibit this kind of profound transformation in her own daily life. This implies that the individual members, each community, and the wider Church must be radically open to the insights, transformation, and renewal offered by the Spirit in ongoing and important ways. The ability of the Church and her members to grow, change, and develop over time into genuine persons and communities serves as the most powerful witness to the triune God whose ultimate purpose is "to make all things new."

The Significance of the Church in the Post-Modern World

If numbers count for anything, then we must judge the Second Vatican Council to have been an overwhelming success. Since the liturgical, theological, and structural reforms of the mid-sixties, the Roman Catholic Church has grown and expanded at unprecedented rates in the modern era. Approaching one billion members at the dawn of a new century, there can be no doubt that the fundamental thrust of the Council toward becoming a genuinely global and world-wide Church has been at least partially realized.[32]

Comprising almost one-sixth of the world's population, the Church is also uniquely poised to influence and shape the future of the broader world in which she shares. In the document *Gaudium et Spes* the council fathers predicted that as the world advanced materially, politically, and technologically, it would yearn ever more deeply for some indication as to the meaning and purpose of history itself and human lives within it.[33] The Church, then, finds itself in a position to actually respond to these questions in a way that impacts history and shapes human culture. The efficacy of the Church's response lies in its ability to represent a genuine alternative to the authentic fears and dangers at the heart of these questions. I am convinced that a concrete realization of communion would signify the most compelling response to the question posed by the post-modern world.

Radical individualism, materialism, and nihilism are often the fruit of the Western capitalism that now penetrates almost every culture on the planet. The Church offers not an alternative economic theory as much as an alternative mode of living, which implicitly challenges the ideological foundations upon which capitalism rests. By offering genuine and concrete examples of communities in communion, the Church can challenge the hegemony of Western cultural imperialism, or at least the most perilous dimensions of it. It is only the actual life of a community that can signify the kind of respect for human dignity and autonomy and the broader aspirations of the human spirit that are left unfulfilled by many aspects of contemporary culture. The pervasive loneliness and recurrent feelings of despair that characterize so many expressions of post-modern culture can only be adequately addressed through the manifestations of genuine communities that unite diverse and unique people together in a larger frame of reference. The Church responds to the great cry of the heart arising from our world by creating an ever more vibrant community that calls forth the dynamic potential of each person while at the same time drawing those individuals into an ever closer unity with other lives and the source and end of life itself.

Inasmuch as the Church actually represents and signifies this urgent need and deep yearning for community, she will attract the attention, "win over" people, and actually transform history and culture.

For this to happen what is needed first and foremost is deep conversion—*metanoia*—in all Christians. The next step is an actualization of disinterested, self-giving love that calls for mutuality. Nothing is more central to the faith than the New Commandment of love. Therefore, individuals, parishes, dioceses, churches, must enact the New Commandment and all love one another. Without this premise of mutual love any discussion tends to be fruitless, and often becomes reduced to a polarized "us" against "them."

With this as a basis we can look seriously at how the Church can adapt herself to respond to contemporary society. The bishops and other leaders of the Church should give the first example in this conversion, since they have been entrusted with the primary task of handing on the faith. The profound humility and deep openness for self-sacrificing and atoning love that truly characterizes Christian love must shine forth in the willingness of Church leaders (both lay and ordained) to relinquish any worldly power, ambition, and wealth and serve as examples of meekness and kindness in all things—including the exercise of their own office in the Church. An equally complete response of love by the laity will lay the ground for a true communion at various levels in the Church.

This basis of genuine love and communion will serve as a sign of hope to the world and contribute to developing models of government and leadership that are inclusive of all members, calling on and developing the charisms of each person to their fullest degree. (Under the current model, less than one percent of the Church's membership have any influence on decisions made for everyone.) Thus the Church would contribute a unique model of leadership, based on trinitarian love, in a world and at a time when participative forms of government are the norm in many parts of the world. The development of more shared and participative types of government at local diocesan and metropolitan levels to encourage this kind of open, profound, and far-reaching communication, is what Royce describes as essential to the existence of genuine community. This would also contribute to a greater decentralization of the Church, which would avoid many problems and be more in keeping with concerns expressed at Vatican II.

What will this look like in everyday Church life? I am not implying that every doctrine or teaching be put to a plebiscite, but I am contending that for the kind of community life that I have been describing some kind of inclusion in the decision-making process of those effected by decisions is essential. A greater use of synods at every level of the Church strike me as an obvious first step in this process.[34]

It must be kept in mind that throughout her history the Church has known and utilized many different types of organizational structures and government. Within the great Tradition of the Church, there exist many traditions that include, for example, democratic processes and alternative governing models. My own religious order for instance, the Order of Preachers (commonly referred to as Dominicans), has had a constitutional democracy for almost eight hundred years. Our government is organized around the principles of subsidiarity and the full participation of all those who have been initiated and taken life-long vows to the Order. We elect our superiors and then promise obedience to them, and we have legislative processes that create the rules by which we live our common and personal lives. In other words, we offer a tradition of governance that integrates both participation and mutual responsibility with authentic obedience to elected authority and a sense of accountability of each member to the whole and vice versa.

It is also important to reinterpret ordained ministry as a form of service to the community that includes leadership charisms but that does not exhaust them. In other words, while we should view ordained ministers, including bishops, as having an essential share in the practical, pastoral, and administrative dimension of the communal life, we should not assume that they are the ones who solely "possess" the power over this aspect of the Church and then distribute and share it with the rest of the faithful. This is not to relegate the ordained to simply a cultic or sacramental role, but it does imply that their role in the governance follows from and is secondary to their directly sacramental and evangelical tasks. As Congar made clear even before the Council, the sacraments of initiation serve as the foundation and core of the Christian community. All those who have been baptized and fully initiated into the life of Christ share in the responsibility to care for and develop both the internal and external life of the community. The actual governance of the Church needs to be a shared process that includes all of the membership at some basic level. Furthermore, even the most central and significant offices in the community must be held accountable to the wider body of members.

Developing more inclusive processes of governance and decision-making remains the unfinished task of the Second Vatican Council and the challenge for those who envision the Church as a genuine community of communities that sacramentally represents the promise of salvation to the universal community. The integrity of the communal life of the Church will determine its evangelical efficacy in the new emerging global culture. To truly signify the Body of Christ to the post-modern world means that the Church must continually open herself to renewal and reform so that the fullness of life offered to her by the Holy Spirit might be increasingly realized.

Conclusion:
Communion and the Pneumatological Principle

Before the Second Vatican Council, Yves Congar advanced Catholic ecclesiology by insisting that it be grounded on two principles: the hierarchical and the communal. His focus on the communal opened the way for a deeper reflection not only on the role of the laity in the life of the Church but upon the role of the Holy Spirit in forming the nature and mission of the Church.

The critical insight of *Lumen Gentium*, the first Constitution on the Church, was the integration of these two principles into a single new insight that would infuse the rest of the council documents. I have called this insight the pneumatological principle. This principle grounds the Constitution, because it understands the Spirit of Christ as forming all of the members of the Church, individually and as a whole, into Christ's image, literally giving life to his body the Church as a soul gives life to a human body (LG, 7). *Lumen Gentium* distinguishes, but does not separate, the hierarchy from the rest of the community of the Church, by viewing it as a type of community with a special charism within the wider community of the Church. In this sense, the Church is a community of communities sharing various charisms animated by the Spirit in an analogous way that each individual community is composed of and united by the mutual sharing of charisms empowered by the Holy Spirit (LG, 8). The hierarchy is itself a form of service, building up the unity of the whole universal Church. The Holy Spirit guides, directs, and coordinates this activity in union with the greater action creating and deepening bonds of community and bringing differing levels of community into ever wider circles of unity throughout time and history through, among other resources, the use of certain communities as efficacious signs of genuine community.

The source and goal of all the activity of the Spirit is unity: the primordial unity of the triune God and the final unity of God's plan for all creation (LG, 9). For this reason, the pneumatological principle might also be called a principle of communion. God's own Spirit is working for the conscious, visible (sacramental) unity of all Christian communities, so that they may in turn be a source and collaborative partner with the Spirit in working for the greater unity of all human beings and the reconciliation of all things in Christ. As both

Constitutions of the Church make explicitly clear, the Church does not exist for herself or her members but as a service to the world in cooperation with the divine plan of reunion of creation with the creator (LG, 13, GS 44). The Holy Spirit as animating source and divine guide of this ongoing plan of reunion chooses to work through the visible, living, historical community called the Church of Christ to bring about this greater plan. While this plan remains largely a mystery to us, we can know and cooperate with the concrete, historical action of the Spirit in our life, our community, and the community of communities that we call Church. Learning to consciously and freely cooperate with the Spirit is to cultivate a "communion spirituality": to develop activities and behaviors that build up each of the communities that we participate in, and to help these communities in turn to unite with ever wider spheres of communities, in the hope of creating the one community of all creation for which the Holy Spirit strives.

Communion ecclesiology cannot be understood apart from this matrix of pneumatology, community, and sacrament. At Vatican II, the Church consciously interpreted itself in these terms, desiring both to recover its New Testament foundations and to open itself up to a world that desperately needed it as a sign of hope for the future and the possibility for reconciliation and peace. While in some ways freeing it from past narrow and defensive interpretations, the theology of the Church at Vatican II largely renewed the most fundamental ecclesial categories it could draw upon to make sense of its mission to serve as the Body of Christ. This mandate, renewed at every eucharist, impresses itself on generation after generation of Christians as a fundamental form of identity that offers the Church a genuine and coherent account of its life and mission. As the Body of Christ, the Church realizes its need to live a full and rich communal life that values the contribution of each member of the community. It also clarifies the need for its common moral and ethical life to authenticate its claims about its communal identity as representative of Christ himself. Furthermore, by reminding itself that it has the presence of Christ's own Spirit in its individuals and its corporate body, it grasps the member's greater connection to one another, to other Christian communities, to all the communities of faith throughout the world, to the universal community, and to the divine community—the Trinity—that is the source and goal of all communion.

Notes

1. For a more thorough analysis of pneumatology in both the Old and New Testament see Donald Gelpi, *The Divine Mother* (New York: University Press of America, 1984); George Montague, *The Holy Spirit: Growth of a Biblical Tradition* (New York: Paulist, 1976); James D. G. Dunn, *The Christ and the Spirit, Volume 2: Pneumatology* (Grand Rapids, MI: Eerdmans Publishing Co., 1998); and especially Yves Congar, *I Believe in the Holy Spirit*, 3 vol. (New York: Seabury Press: 1983).
2. See Gelpi, *The Divine Mother*, pp. 53-56; Congar, *I Believe in the Holy Spirit*, pp. 49-59.
3. See Gelpi, *The Divine Mother*, pp. 98-99
4. Jerome Murphy-O'Connor. *Becoming Human Together* (Wilmington, DE: Michael Glazier, 1982) 183.
5. See also Raymond Brown, *The Community of the Beloved Disciple* (New York, Paulist Press, 1979).
6. Cf. John Clendenning, *The Life and Thought of Josiah Royce* (Madison, WI: University of Wisconsin Press, 1980); Robert V. Hine, *Josiah Royce: From Grass Valley to Harvard* (Norman, OK: University of Oklahoma Press, 1991); Bruce Kuklick, *Josiah Royce: An Intellectual Biography* (Indianapolis, IN: Bobbs-Merrill, 1972); Frank Oppenheim, Josiah Royce's "Intellectual Development," *Idealistic Studies* 6 (1976), 85-104.
7. Josiah Royce, *The Problem of Christianity* (Chicago: University of Chicago Press) 194. Hereafter referred to as PC.
8. Letter to Mary Whiton Calkins, *Letters,* 646.
9. Ibid.
10. PC, 236-238.
11. PC, 239-240.
12. PC, 243.
13. PC, 244.
14. PC, 248-249.
15. PC, 253.
16. PC, 255-256.
17. PC, 256–257.
18. PC, 264.
19. PC, 265.
20. PC, 270.
21. Charles Sanders Peirce, *Collected Papers, Vol. 5* (Cambridge, MA: Belknap Press of Harvard University Press, 1965). Joseph Brent, *C.S. Peirce: A Life* (Indianapolis, IN: Indiana University Press, 1993). Bruce Kuklick, *The Rise of American Philosophy* (New Haven, CT: Yale University Press, 1977). Bruce Kuklick, *History of Philosophy in America* (Oxford: Clarendon Press, 2001). Donald Gelepi, *Varieties of Transcendental Experience* (Collegeville, MN: Liturgical Press, 2000), 227–288.
22. Peirce actually develops his entire system of logic based on the "science of signs" (*Collected Papers*, vol. 3, par. 149; vol. 2, par. 227ff).

23. I owe much of my analysis and summary of these three types of signs to Terrence Hawkes, *Structuralism and Semiotics* (Berkeley, CA: University of California Press, 1977) 122–150.

24. *Catechism of the Catholic Church*, #1127.

25. See Thomas Aquinas, *Summa Theologiae*, III, Q. 60, art. 3. Much of my analysis of signs here is based on this article and Thomas' subsequent commentary on this article in explaining the various sacraments.

26. Vorgrimler, *Sacramental Theology* (Collegeville, MN: Liturgical Press, 1992) 30-32; Karl Rahner, *Encyclopedia of Theology* (New York: Seabury Press, 1975) 1477–1488. But symbol does not adequately translate the full meaning of sacrament into English as it does not connote enough. Things in English can be "mere" symbols. That is why I propose Peirce's tri-partitite analysis as signs for which symbol is one type, but Sacrament is a special type of sign that includes all three types of signs in a unique relationship.

27. See especially Vorgrimler; for a basic introduction to the seven sacraments see Joseph Martos, *Doors to the Sacred* (New York: Image Books, 1982); *The Catechism of the Catholic Church*, para. 1210–1690; and Richard McBrien, *Catholicism* (San Francisco: Harper Collins Publishers, 1994) 805–879.

28. I am especially grateful here to the remarkable scholarship of my colleague Sarah Fairbanks, O.P., Ph. D., and to her dissertation entitled, *Foundations for a Roman Catholic Theology of the Laity and the Ministry of the Word in Selected Documents of Vatican II* (Ann Arbor, Michigan: University of Michigan Press, 2002).

29. Fairbanks, 164.

30. See John Paul II, *At the Beginning of the New Millennium*, 43, where, speaking about the spirituality of communion, he writes: "Let us have no illusions: unless we follow this spiritual path, external structures of communion will serve very little purpose. They will become mechanisms without a soul, 'masks' of communion rather than means of expression and growth."

31. Cf. John Paul II, *Ut Unum Sint* (May 25, 1995) para. 4. *Origins* 25 (June 8, 1995), 4.

32. In the last major U. N. Study, *World Population Prospects: The 1994 Revisions* (1995). The number of Roman Catholics was estimated at 968,025,000. Most demographic studies conducted since this U.N. study suggest that the Catholic Church is continuing to grow at rates that will easily take it over a billion members by the millennium and will keep it growing afterward.

33. GS, 9-10.

34. For further reflection on this point see the compelling discussion of local synods and the responsibility of the bishop in J.M.R. Tillard's *Church of Churches: The Ecclesiology of Communion*, transl. R. C. De Preaux (Collegeville, MN, 1992), 215-230.

Chapter 4

The Church as the Sacrament
of Communion for the World

The theoretical dualism that reigned in the Church from the time of Augustine (discussed in chapter 1) presented for Christians two profound problems, which finally had to be addressed at Vatican II. First, the complexities of ordinary human life make it difficult to maintain the clear distinctions that theories provide. As Congar observed, ordinary Christians experienced more and more that the spiritual and temporal spheres were profoundly connected. As they were striving to respond to the gospel, people were unable to live "dualistic" lives. Christianity led the faithful (ordinary Christians, mystics and theologians, bishops and priests) to conclude that grace suffused the whole of human experience, and that no dimension of human life was "off limits" to God's saving action and self-communicating presence. Second, the gospel command for evangelization and Christ's own example of limitless mercy and compassion dramatically contradicted the fatalistic and rigidly dualistic understanding of the Church that had emerged over the centuries. In the light of the Gospels, and the letters of Paul, it became strikingly clear that the Church exists to serve the world by proclaiming the gospel in hopes of repentance, conversion, and salvation. The disciples of Christ are specifically instructed to go out "to all the world" (Mt 28:19) and proclaim the good news of salvation. In the light of the resurrection, Paul argues, there is no longer "Jew nor Greek, slave nor free, woman nor man" (Gal 3:14). All humanity has become a "new creation" brought about by the resurrection and Christ's giving over of his Spirit. This ultimately called into question Augustine's bleak analysis and clarified the narrow context from which he was writing.

Lumen Gentium and *Gaudium et Spes:* The Constitutions of the Church in the World

From the beginning of the Second Vatican Council, the scope and outlook of the council fathers was completely different from that of the besieged bishop in Northern Africa at the end of the patristic era. They desired to break out of the dualism that confined the Church to an otherworldly and merely spiritual realm of existence and concern. They realized that the dynamics of grace and God's plan of salvation revealed in Christ meant that there were not two worlds but one. In composing the first official Constitutions of the Church, the council fathers agreed that there exists only one fundamental realm of human existence, pervaded mysteriously by the powers of grace as well as sin, but with one single destiny: the reign of God. While having a special and unique role to play, the Church does not represent a separate or parallel dimension of life. She exists as part of this world, and the world's and her destiny are genuinely tied. The council fathers saw the Church not as an ark protecting the patrimony of the past and safely floating the blessed out of the city of humans' chaos. Rather, they considered her as an efficacious sign, a sacrament, of Christ himself, who gives his own life in service to the human city so that it might have everlasting life and be freed from the chaos and sin that threaten to engulf it (LG, 1).

As pointed out earlier, the second paragraph of *Lumen Gentium* sets the theological framework for the Constitutions, explaining the mystery of the Trinity and the missions of the persons of the Trinity toward creation. In this context, human history is understood as a process of life, created out of the internal dynamics of the shared life and love of the persons of the Trinity. Humans can freely choose to participate in this life. While the option of human freedom can create disorder and chaos in the world, and lead human beings away from God, God chooses to continue reaching out and seek to bring all people back into a loving relationship with one another and the divine life. The extent to which God desires to lead all history back to its divine origins is revealed in the missions of the Son and the Holy Spirit, who enter and shape history in a powerful new way. Jesus Christ, the divine/human person, unites God and human beings in a unique way and inaugurates the reign of God, which is the name Jesus gives to God's plan for the destiny of history. When human beings reject Jesus Christ, God reveals the fullness of his love by raising him from the dead. This represents not a single mysterious vindication of Jesus' life but the first sign of *new* life—the new future—that awaits all people open to Christ's proclamation of God's reign.

The gift of his own Spirit—which is in fact the Spirit of God—is the other remarkable fruit of the resurrection. So, far from abandoning sinful, and now murderous, humanity, God makes human history his own. God unites it with the divine life not just in Christ but in an ongoing way through the gift of the Spirit, which will reach to the ends of the earth, transforming the world toward God's final destiny.

Within this context the Church finds its own identity. Jesus Christ plants the seed of the Church through his own life, ministry, and proclamation of the reign of God. In the resurrection, the risen Lord appears to those who knew him in his lifetime. He fills them with his own Spirit that they may literally become his body: a visible sign of his continuing presence in history. They are not only given his Spirit but also his mission to preach the reign of God and to authenticate its existence through their shared life and practical ethical behavior. The Church emerged out of the Paschal Mystery: the life, death, and resurrection of Jesus and the sending of his Holy Spirit on his disciples. The Paschal Mystery unites the destinies of Church and world in a dramatic way. Like Jesus himself, the Church exists to reveal to the world her divine origins, the love of God that sustains and desires it, giving each life ultimate meaning and fulfillment. The Church also serves the world by offering it, through the mystery of grace, a fore-taste and vision of the destiny that awaits all humanity in the future reign of God. However, the Paschal Mystery also humbles the Church by reminding her both of the limitations imposed upon her by human sinfulness and history itself, and of the fact that the final victory of love in history will be the result of a supernatural and mysterious miracle of divine mercy and re-creation, which the Church, like the rest of humanity, will only be able to receive gratefully.

The Church as a "Sure Seed of Unity, Hope, and Salvation for the Whole Human Race"

The above quote, taken from *Lumen Gentium* 9, sets the agenda for both Constitutions on the Church. While the Pastoral Constitution would deal explicitly with matters of the Church's direct analysis of and service to the contemporary world, the Dogmatic Constitution itself defines the inner life of the Church in terms of its mission to proclaim salvation and signify the unity offered by Christ. Original Sin disconnected human beings from God and one another, and replaced genuine communion with false bonds of self-interest, envy, greed, and all types of misunderstanding and conflict. This breakdown of authentic, uniting, relationships, over time has led to a crisis of trust, fidelity, and confidence both in human beings and the institutions they created to maintain order and unity among people. Consequently, the meaning and value of human life itself has been called into question and even negated by the chaos of this radical division and conflict. In the light of this general discord, the Church offers a ray of hope and a chance for re-establishing the original unity and common purpose of life that God gave the world. In creating the Church as his own body—a mutual inter-dependence and shared life of many unique and diverse parts—Christ offered the world an example of the unity it sought through both personal relationships and institutional forms. The Dogmatic Constitution attempts to articulate this vision of Christ in a theological and practical manner, but always with an eye toward the need for authentic unity at every level of ecclesial life. For this reason, communion emerged not only as one goal among many but as the organizing concept and driving vision for both Constitutions on the Church. As suggested by Congar and Hamer (among other theologians) before the Council, it became clear that the term not only suggested a newer, more inclusive understanding of the Church's membership but also connoted its universal mission to work for reconciliation and unity among all God's people.

Communion, while rich in connotations, points to the need for individuals to belong to communities that are in turn united with other communities, in wider and wider circles of unity. For Christians, the final goal of this ever-widening circle is the divine community—the triune life of God who is love, that is, a communion of love. The purpose of the Church, in fact, resides precisely in facilitating, as an instrument of the Holy Spirit, this divine process of re-uniting all people into the universal community. This is why internal communion is such an essential dimension of the Dogmatic Constitution. The Church's efficacy as a sign and witness to the divine plan rests on her own ability to achieve a genuine and visible common life. The Church's own communion becomes a sign and source of wider possibilities of communion, both inside and outside the visible boundaries of the Christian Church.

The Role of the Church in the Post-Modern and Hyper-Modern World

Gaudium et Spes describes the modern world largely in terms of change: from a stable social order to a more fluid and "unstable" political and economic environment, driven primarily by growth in industry and technology. Another dramatic change at the roots of society occurred in terms of the Church's and religion's role in the social ethos. With the dawn of the Enlightenment, European society became relatively secular and fundamentally re-orientated toward the ideals and thought-forms of scientific theory as the foundational patterns of viewing the world. Modernity connotes the experience of a society that believes in the positive value of change itself and sees in it the hope of progress, growth, and the development of a higher standard of living for everyone. Modernity, as a type of culture in itself, values change for its own sake, understanding both the immense possibilities and dangers inherent in this phenomenon. Nevertheless, modern culture accepts the inevitability of change in light of the technological, social, and political forces that science and economics demand.

In many ways, *Gaudium et Spes* remains extremely relevant today, as most of the world is still experiencing modernity either in its initial or fully developed stages. What we commonly refer to as the "third" or "developing" world is in fact a world that is in many ways coming to terms with its own unique forms of modernity. The positive and negative dimensions of this reality are well examined and interpreted in the text of the Constitution. On the other hand, in many parts of Europe and the "first world," most scholars and commentators feel that they are no longer experiencing modernity in a strict sense. They have described this new reality as "post-modernity." Similarly, I would argue that the United States is not really modern, nor post-modern, but is experiencing its own variation on this foundational cultural pattern, which I will call "hyper-modern."

European commentators/philosophers almost inevitably describe post-modernism as a "radical break" from the Enlightenment concept that the world has order, purpose, and direction, which can be known and controlled through human intelligence and cooperation.[1] For Europeans, the twentieth century at first created a crisis for this world view and then shattered it altogether. Post-modernism connotes the attempt to pick up the pieces and shape a new, and less ambitious, view of reality. It rejects the naïve optimism of modernism that uncritically accepted the notion that progress and growth were necessarily implied in change, and that science and economics were basically positive forces underlying and guiding change itself. Post-modernism is skeptical not just of religion and the other dimensions of the stable world order that modernism supplanted, it is skeptical of modernism itself and has not found any world view or foundational way of thinking that can "fill the void"—indeed it doubts whether such a foundational world view exists at all.

In many ways, American culture, though rooted in many different and competing varieties of European cultures, did not emerge as fully cohesive and "modern" until the early to mid-nineteenth century. Somewhat owing to the work of American philosopher Albert Borgmann,[2] I would propose three foundational sources of modern American culture: 1) the adoption of the American Constitution and especially the ratification of the Bill of Rights in 1791; 2) the Louisiana Purchase in 1803 and the massive territorial expansion that it enabled; 3) the development of large-scale national industrial corporations in all sectors of economic production between 1800 and 1850 in the Northeastern and Midwestern parts of the United States, and the massive agricultural production in the South, made possible by the extensive dependence on slavery. These three sources combined to create a uniquely American culture that represented the dawn of a new epoch in Western history. A great deal has been written on the unique character of the culture in the last twenty years, and yet as early as 1840 it was recognized as a new moment in history by Alexis de Tocqueville.[3] While it would be impossible to adequately describe the scope and breadth of this culture here, I would generally characterize it as prizing two dominant values: individuality and growth.

Like its other "first-world" counterparts, I think that America is experiencing a cultural crisis, but one that is actually quite different from what is experienced in Europe. It is hyper-modern not because the American form of modernism has somehow broken down or failed. On the contrary, hyper-modernism asserts that American modernism has succeeded all too well. Its very success has in fact created the crisis that American culture now confronts. With the development of newer and more refined levels of technology, the speed of growth has begun to outstrip the human ability to adapt to the environmental, biological, and psychological changes that it brings.[4] Similarly, the increasingly fierce emphasis on individuality has led to an ideological individualism that has severed the person from his or her various communities during a period when individuals were discovering more than ever the vital need for other people in their lives. American hyper-modern culture has led to an important and very precarious new phenomenon in this society: hyper-individualism. I will try to explain.

Americans are fascinated with the idea of community, and the term serves as a very significant "buzzword" in American culture. Research conducted in the last decades of the twentieth century showed that community represented the single most urgent longing of Americans, and also, importantly, the one goal that seemed most elusive and difficult to attain.[5] On the one hand, they yearn to be socially connected and united at a very fundamental level in their lives. On the other hand, Americans embrace a type of radical individualism that seems to negate the possibility of achieving the genuine social bonds that they desire. In many ways this ongoing dialectic between individual and community has defined the cultural development of American society.

From the beginning, the ideals of individuality and community have existed in a creative tension that has driven the development of dual, and often competing, social foci. The Constitution of the country itself tried to put forth a model of government that would safeguard the "sanctity" of the individual, individual free choice, and the search for personal autonomy, while also insuring that some levels of unity and social identity are maintained to protect the common good of all citizens. Striking and maintaining a working balance between personal freedom and social order for the advancement of the whole country became the task of the government that developed in the aftermath of the American Revolution.[6] The liberal capitalistic underpinnings of the economic order also depend on a competition between individual ambition and ingenuity and communal organization and restraints that direct the individual drive in a way that actually advances the whole. The Calvinistic Protestant roots of the civic religion also stressed the primacy of individual faith and salvation over against the social necessity of religious institutions.[7] The ideology of individualism that emerges out of the political and social developments of the eighteenth and nineteenth centuries in America comes to fruition in the twentieth century in a culture that reifies the individual and focuses the lens of its attention on the quest for personal fulfillment and self-expression.

This exaltation of the individual (hyper-individualism) has two primary consequences. First, the ongoing competition between individuals and the need for personal self-fulfillment, even at the expense of other people and significant social bonds, takes a toll on both those that succeed at this process and those that fail. The ideology of hyper-individualism tends to isolate the person and create a sense of loneliness and alienation at deep levels in the human psyche.[8] This means that society not only nurtures individualism but must also try to ameliorate its negative effects. The society, and the individual communities within it, must inevitably take on a therapeutic function, offering care and refuge for lonely, emotionally battered individuals. Secondly, the need and desire for community, while not lost, become subordinated to the emphasis on the individual. Community, as a matter of fact, becomes an important means for individual self-expression and personal growth. The question is whether genuine community can be achieved or maintained by individuals who participate in it mostly for selfish reasons. In other words, the quandary in contemporary America is that individuals seek communal and social experiences to overcome the isolation and loneliness that often accompany the quest for personal ambition and self-fulfillment, but the bonds necessary to create community itself cannot exist if all its potential members remain solely motivated by self-interest.

In America, the term community is so vague that it can refer to any number of social configurations: anything from a church to a local civic club, from any kind of organization to a special gathering of people at a sports stadium—practically any social encounter that makes an impact on one's personal consciousness. Nevertheless, that people seem to continually seek community remains an irrefutable aspect of American culture. The question then arises as to what actually constitutes a genuine and authentic community, and how individuals can find and experience it in a way that preserves their legitimate desire for personal autonomy and self-expression. Robert Bellah, an important social researcher and commentator, has suggested that it falls to religious institutions to offer a model of community that can both attract and nurture individuals and challenge the ideology of radical individualism that pervades our culture.[9] Bellah contends that Christianity offers a long tradition of embodying community that unites the twin foci of the American culture legacy. It falls to the individual churches, and to their united effort, to fully recover the Christian communal dimension as a counter-cultural alternative to the inadequate and temporary models of community that arise out of hyper-individualism.

The Church as communion has something significant to offer to those in the modern, post-modern, and hyper-modern worlds. The Church of Christ, as a universal Church, must encounter the world in all its various stages of development, must both listen and learn from each culture, and challenge it to conversion with the message of the gospel with which it has been entrusted. To those parts of the world confronting modernity in all its various stages, the profound anthropological and social analysis of *Gaudium et Spes* remains as relevant today as it was during the twentieth century, when it was written in response to and reflection on almost three hundred years of experience with this cultural reality in Europe. The Constitution's understanding of a number of crucial matters offers a rational, prudent, hopeful, and genuinely humane guide for all people of good will. These include: the right relationship between the genuine autonomy of the individual and the common good of the wider community; the centrality of family life; the sacredness of work and human labor; the rights of all human beings to basic forms of justice; human rights and the role of the Church as agent uniting the multiple dimensions of human life, defending the rights of all human beings, and pointing to the sacred and deeper meaning of life, which offers right order even amidst change. With profound realism the Constitution seeks to offer a uniquely Christian, and fully human, analysis of the possibilities and dangers of cultures in the midst of great change. Under the guidance of the Holy Spirit at work in every dimension of life, human beings are longing to live in communities of memory and hope that offer them meaning and direction for their own lives and those of their families. It falls not only to the Church but to all people of good will to unite and create communities of justice and love. These can grow in ever greater union until the day when all human beings are brought together to fulfill the vision of the community of communities, which is at the heart of not only Christianity but of all religious and genuinely loving peoples of the earth.

The other fundamental Constitution on the Church, *Lumen Gentium*, as it is progressively and more profoundly understood and implemented in the years to come, will also serve as a tremendous resource for the Church's attempt to genuinely engage modern, post-modern, and hyper-modern cultures simultaneously. The rich concept of communion, which is at the heart of *Lumen Gentium*, offers the potential to make the Church itself an authentic sign, an engaging and efficacious model (a sacrament in reality) of what true hope and human value may look like to cultures desperate for just such examples. In modern cultures, the value of individual work and the sacredness of human rights and traditions must be upheld against the onslaught of economic pressures and social transformations that can improve but also impoverish the lives of multitudes of people. In post-modern societies, the Church can offer the possibility of purpose and direction to human life, not as an absolute, completed, and indubitable conclusion, but as an open-ended, yet Spirit-guided plan, for the salvation of humanity in spite of and in triumph over suffering, tragedy, and death. To the post-modern world the Church offers an invitation to become reacquainted with a God who reveals himself as both human being and compassionate and animating Spirit, who involves human beings in the building of the reign of God, announced and embodied in the life of Jesus Christ. The Church acts no longer as one more self-interested and politically motivated state competing with other political and economic entities, nor is it a separate entity existing alongside, but ultimately above, this world. Rather, the Church is deeply and profoundly involved in this world as an agent of the divine Spirit of Christ, who is intent on drawing it together into ever greater levels of community and bringing about genuine justice, peace, and unity to and between all nations and peoples of the earth. The Church as a communion opens up an opportunity for a re-connection with post-modernity, giving both a chance to start a new vital relationship with the other, offering a way out of the dizzying cycle of hopelessness, sorrow, and alienation that is at the heart of the lost dream of modernity and the end of the pre-Vatican II Eurocentric Church.

The Church as a communion answers the "cry of the heart" of hyper-modernity. American culture in particular is in desperate need of genuine and authentic models of community that can answer the American desire for full individuality and autonomy while at the same time uniting the individual in a full sharing of life with other people. The Vatican II vision of communion offers just such an understanding of community. Furthermore, the Church can demonstrate how individuals can participate in various kinds and levels of community simultaneously, beginning with the most basic one: the family. The Church itself exists as a community of communities and draws the individuals who belong to her into this rich, complex, and ultimately universal community of relationships. This vast broadening of the scope of the individual's personal life pulls him or her out of the narcissism and self-centered illusions of American individualism and helps that person to see and make a commitment to a community much greater than oneself. This kind of broader vision also enables both individuals and communities to "see through" many of the false allures of capitalism and consumerism and desire to work for higher values of social justice and human rights that the Church teaches and attempts to embody.

In all these cultures, communion cannot just be an idea that the Church teaches or an ideal that she strives for as a distant possibility. Communion must be an efficacious sign that truly "speaks" in a direct and powerful way to both the believers and non-believers throughout these various and diverse societies. This great task of evangelization is not an option, for it was entrusted to us by Jesus Christ himself. This mission can only be accomplished, the Council believed, by a Church that truly lives as the Mystical Body of Christ. To fulfill this vision, Vatican II called the Church to be a community of communities, filled with and empowered by the Spirit of God, enlivened by the sharing of gifts and charisms in such a way that she acts as both a sign and an instrument of God's saving plan for the universal community. Spirit, community, and sacrament are the component parts of the foundation laid by the Second Vatican Council for the Church in the new millennium. Vatican II is not over; in many ways, it has only just begun. The Church will need to spend much of the twenty-first century trying to truly interpret and realize the vision of communion laid out in its Constitutions. To convert the structures of an ancient institution and to attune the hearts and minds of a billion people would seem like an impossible task if it were merely a human endeavor. However, our understanding of communion itself means that the Spirit of God will take the leading and guiding role. This is the mystical and mysterious dimension of our life as the Body of Christ—along with the greatest human effort, and often in spite of the greatest human inertia and resistance, things do change in the life of the Church. The Church truly is a living, breathing body, and it grows, changes, and develops over time. That the divine Spirit chooses to co-operate with us in this life is most mysterious and surprising, but it cannot be denied or ignored. For our part we must join in the effort, and each community must strive to live in true communion so as to advance the reign of God and truly fulfill our function within the wider body, the community of communities, the Church.

No one knows what the Church will look like in one hundred years. Clearly, it will go through many changes. Yet, these changes will not be random, nor should they be driven by ideology or arbitrary innovation. The Church has Constitutions that are thorough, theologically coherent, and profoundly connected with her tradition. Nevertheless, as is the case for all Constitutions, the task remains to interpret and implement them according to the changing and various needs of the times and the situations that the Church experiences. If at the heart of any structural change this sense of communion remains firmly rooted and enhanced, then many different models of Church organization and institutional design are conceivable. The government of the Church is a human creation that, while guided by the Spirit and necessary for community life, is not central or primary to the life of communion, as we have seen. Hopefully, some of the clarifications offered in this book might be helpful in determining those things that are fundamental and necessary to communion and those that are open to change, development, and revision.

The goal of Vatican II was not change but fidelity; fidelity to the Spirit of Christ, who was calling it to a new era of life as a world-wide community in the "global village." Vatican II was also attempting to be faithful to the gospel and the life of Christ narrated there, which it seeks to imitate and embody in this world. Similarly, in a humble and small way this book has sought to be faithful to these same criteria. Whether great or small, heroic or humble, the Spirit of Christ insures that all faithful efforts are part of God's universal plan to unite everything in heaven and earth in Christ. This hope, this truth, lies at the heart of the complex and fascinating term that we call "communion."

Notes

1. See particularly Jean-Francois Lyotard, *The Post-Modern Condition: A Report on Knowledge*, transl. Geoff Bennington and Brian Massumi, foreword by Frederic Jameson (Minneapolis, MN: University of Minnesota Press, 1984); Frederic Jameson, *The Cultural Turn: Selected Writings on the Post-Modern, 1983-1998* (London: Verso, 1998).
2. Ibid.
3. Alexis de Tocqueville, *Democracy in America*, 4 vols. (Garden City, NY: Doubleday, 1969).
4. See Albert Borgmann, *Technology and the Character of Contemporary Life* (Chicago: University of Chicago Press, 1984).
5. Bellah, Robert, et al, *Habits of the Heart* (Berkeley, CA: University of California Press, 1985). Gelpi, Donald, ed., *Beyond Individualism* (Notre Dame, IN: University of Notre Dame Press, 1989). Fowler, Robert Booth, *The Dance With Community* (Lawrence, KS: University of Kansas Press, 1991).
6. Unger, Roberto Mangabeira, *Knowledge and Politics* (New York: The Free Press, 1975). Sullivan, William, *Reconstructing Public Philosophy* (Berkeley, CA: University of California Press, 1986).
7. Bellah, Robert, *The Broken Covenant* (New York: Seabury Press, 1975).
8. Borgmann, *Crossing the Post-Modern Divide*, 44.
9. Bellah, Robert, "Religion and the Shape of National Culture" in *America* (vol. 181, number 3), 9-14.

Acknowledgments

I would like to thank all of the staff at New City Press and especially Gary Brandl for working so hard to make this book possible. I would also like to thank Frank Oveis whose wise advice sent me in their direction in the first place.

This book was written primarily with the help, input, and encouragement of the John Courtney Murray Writers Group, and I am deeply grateful to all of its members for their devotion to our common endeavor over the years and the special counsel that they gave me on this book. I would especially like to thank the Jesuit Community at Berkeley for hosting us so graciously during the summers. Alex Garcia-Rivera, Nancy Pineda-Madrid, Robert Lasalle-Klein, Dan Groody and Si Hendry were especially helpful friends and colleagues. Special mention must be made here of the profound influence and deep gratitude I have toward Frank Oppenheim for his many years of tireless work and his willingness to share so much accumulated wisdom with me. Greg Zuschlag has been an invaluable friend, assistant, editor, and collaborator without whom this book would have never come to completion. Patricia Bruno was always there to offer encouragement, practical advice, and companionship. I must offer a special note of thanks to the two great intellectual and vocational influences on my life: Tom O'Meara, who first opened my eyes to the great possibilities of theology and my vocation as a Dominican, and Don Gelpi, who has been my mentor and guide over the last fourteen years, as I have tried to faithfully serve God and the Church as a theologian and preacher.

Finally, I need to thank my brother Pat, who worked so diligently on this project with me from the very beginning, and whose own example of life illustrates so profoundly what this book is about.

Index

A

Acts of the Apostles, 109–112, 114–115, 122
America, American culture, 32, 135, 176–179, 181–182
Ananias and Sapphira, 111
anointing of the sick, 156–157
apostles, 67–68
    see also specific names, topics, and events
Apostolicam Actuositatem, 81–82
Augustine, Saint, 27–29, 170–171
authority, *see* hierarchy; leadership

B

baptism, 62, 135, 145, 156–157, 165
    call to holiness, 75–77
    charisms, 95
    non-Catholics and, 80
believers, *see* Christians
Bellah, Robert, 179
Bellarmine, Robert, 31
Bible, *see* scripture
bishop(s), 67–73, 75, 145–147
    of Rome, 68, 147, 161
Body of Christ, 59, 96, 108, 115, 119, 155, 159
    and Mystical Body of Christ, 44
    People of God and, 62
    in post-modern world, 165–168

C

Cain, city of, 27–29
call to holiness, 75–77, 95
Catholicism, *see* Roman Catholic Church
charisms, 59, 63–64, 77, 81, 95, 164
    leaders and, 71, 145–146, 165
    pneumatology and, 119–122
    sharing in community, 108, 114–115, 124, 142, 166, 182
    three essential, 138–140
charity, 63, 93
    see also love
choice, human, *see* freedom

chosen people, the, 61
Christ, *see* Jesus Christ
Christians, Christian Church, 77, 94, 140–142, 155, 174
    attitudes and conduct, 112, 114–115, 124–125, 180
    as Body of Christ, *see* Body of Christ
    Christ and Holy Spirit in, 106–109
    see also Holy Spirit; Jesus Christ
    Church of Christ, the one, *see* Church of Christ
    community as goal, *see* community
    cooperation among, 60, 62, 80, 91–94, 160–161
    defining, 85–86
    discipleship, 79, 170–171
    ecumenicism, 160–161
    image and likeness of Jesus, 87–88, 106, 113
    mission of, 66
    non-Christians, relationship with, *see* non-Christians
    as People of God, *see* People of God
    Protestant, 30–31
    Roman Catholics as, *see* Roman Catholic Church
    see also conversion; spirituality; specific topics
Christus Dominus, 81
Church, Christian, *see* Church of Christ
Church, Roman Catholic, *see* Roman Catholic Church
Church of Christ, 80, 96, 140–143, 179
    as community of communities, *see under* community
    Roman Catholic Church and, 143
    see also Body of Christ; Christians; People of God
City of God, The, 27–29
co-dependence, 139
communication, 133–134
communion, 29, 168, 174, 180
    Church as, 46–50, 56, 159–160, 179–184
    and community, terminology, 95–97
    the sacrament of, *see* eucharist

triad of, 100–168
  see also community; Holy Spirit;
    sacrament/sacramentality
Communion Pneumatology, 124–126
community (-ies), 29, 46–48, 96–97,
  162–163, 168
  authentic, 179–183
  Christianity, as fundamental to,
    76, 85–89, 94–95, 111–112,
    118
  and communion, terminology,
    96–97
  of communities, 143–144, 147,
    180, 182
    see also Body of Christ
  divine (final goal), 174
  Holy Spirit as fostering, 58–59,
    62, 122–126, 149, 157
  individual life and, 129–133,
    177–179
    see also individuality
  of interpretation, 149–150
  "members one of another,"
    126–147
  Royce, Josiah on, 127–138
  sharing gifts, 87–89
    see also charisms
  sinners as comprising, 60
  see also People of God; unity
confirmation, 135, 156–157
Congar, Yves, O.P., 30–31, 44–48, 56,
  166, 170, 174
Constitutions on the Church, 53–96,
  171–174, 180–181
conversion, 93, 117–119, 122–123,
  157, 163
Council of Trent, 28–30
Councils, Vatican, *see* Vatican I;
  Vatican II
Counter-Reformation, 29–32, 44, 102
covenant, the new, 61, 114, 140
creation, 58, 61, 81
  God's plan for, 66, 83, 117, 122,
    167
culture(s), cultural diversity, 81–84, 92
  "interculturation mandate,"
    64–65

D

deacons, 73
Dignitatus Humanae, 82–84
discipleship, Christian, 79, 170–171
diversity, recognition of, 81–84
  "interculturation mandate," 64–65
divine plan, *see under* God

Dogmatic Constitution on the Church,
  see Lumen Gentium
dualism, 27–29, 34–35, 85, 170–171

E

ecclesiology (-ies)
  of the Constitutions on the
    Church, 53–96
  development of, 43
  and pneumatology, 49–50
  before Vatican II, 30–35
    see also specific names, topics,
      descriptions
economics, 162–163, 181
ecumenicism, 160–161
enemies, love of, 114–115
Enlightenment, the, 175–176
episcopacy, episcopal consecration, *see*
  bishops
eucharist, 47–48, 55, 59, 63, 72, 135,
  142, 145, 156–157, 167–168
Europe, European culture, 175–176,
  179–180
evangelization, 62, 75, 93, 141,
  170–171, 182

F

faith, 83
family life, 63, 92, 182
  see also community
forgiveness, 114–115
  see also reconciliation
freedom, 83, 93, 172
  of religion, 82–84

G

Gaudium et Spes, 80–94, 96–98,
  124–125, 162, 171–175, 179–180
Gentiles, 61–62
gifts, *see* charisms
God, 61–62
  city of, 27–29
  love of, 116–117, 172–174
  mystery of, 58, 116–117
  plan of, 66, 83–84, 122, 125, 184
    see also Trinity; specific topics
gospel, proclaiming, *see* evangelization
Gospels, 170–171
  see also specific Gospels
government, 164–166

grace, 34, 76, 79, 117, 170
    community and, 123, 137
    gifts of, *see* charisms
    Holy Spirit, as presence of, *see* Holy Spirit
    non-Christians and, 64–65, 88, 91
    see also salvation

H

Hamer, Jerome, O.P., 48–50, 56, 174
hierarchy, Catholic Church, 41–42, 49, 60, 66–73, 81
hierarchical principle, 47
    and leadership, 163–166
history
    God's ongoing presence, 61, 97
    human, 27–29, 97, 171–173
holiness, call to, 75–77, 95
holy orders, 156–157
Holy Spirit, 85–86, 94, 102–126, 148, 167, 172, 182–184
    in all people, 64–65, 81, 88, 125, 157
    and the Church, 42, 49, 58–59, 67–68, 75, 77, 98, 121–126, 159
    ecclesiology of, *see* pneumatology
    Pentecost, 46, 68, 110–111
    unity, as fostering, 46–47, 62, 122–126, 149, 166–167
    see also Trinity; specific topics
humankind
    dignity of, 82–84, 87–88, 93, 162–163
    God's plan for, 66, 83–84, 167
    history of, 27–29, 97, 171–173
    the Incarnation and, 87–88
    nature of, 61, 86–89, 93, 96
hymns, 156–157

I

icon(s), 150–151, 154, 156, 158
    Church as, 155–156, 159–161
index(es), 151, 154–159
individuality, 40
    and community, *see* community
    individualism, 128, 137–138, 162, 176–179, 182
initiation, sacrament of, 74–76, 135, 142, 165
"interculturation mandate," 64–65
Islamic people, *see* non-Christians
Israel, 61

J

Jesus Christ, 154–155, 172
    and the Holy Spirit, *see* Holy Spirit; *pneuma*
    image and likeness of, 87–88, 106, 113
    imitation of, 76, 115, 138–140
    the new covenant, 61, 114, 140
    the Paschal Mystery, *see* Paschal Mystery
    resurrection of, 104–106, 113, 170–172
    salvation as from, 79, 107
    second coming of, 141, 157
    threefold office of, 62–64
    truth of, 112–113
    see also pneuma; Trinity; specific topics
Jesus Christ and the Church, 30, 41–42, 49, 58–59, 67
    Church as icon, 159–161
    see also Body of Christ
Jews, 61–62, 135
    see also non-Christians
John, Gospel of, 112–115, 126
justice, 93

K

kingdom of Christ, 62, 64
kingdom of God, 140
    see also grace
koinonia, 126

L

laity, 41–42, 46–47, 74–75, 81–82, 92, 163
    pre-Vatican II, 39
leadership, 163–166
liturgy, 54–60, 63
local church, 28–29, 69–70, 72, 96, 145
love, 42, 49, 59, 75, 163–164
    community and, 140
    of enemies, 114–115
    of God for us, 116–117, 172–174
    as "loyalty to loyalty," 136–137
loyalty, 139
    love and, 136–137
Luke, Gospel of, 109–112, 114–115
Lumen Gentium, 53–54, 56–82, 94, 124, 166, 171–174, 180–181

M

mankind, *see* humankind
marriage, 63, 92, 156–157
martyrs, in community, 139–140
Mary, mother of Jesus, 78–80
metanoia, see conversion
ministry, Christian, 111–112
ministry, ordained, 165
mission of the Church, 28, 55, 58, 64–65, 75, 87, 167–168
mission of Jesus, extending, 97–98
modern world (the Church in), 27–29, 32–35, 55, 64–65, 75
    Gaudium et Spes, 84–94
    and post-modern world, 162–166, 174–184
Möhler, Johann Adam, 32, 35–37, 45, 49, 57, 95
mystery of the Church, 46–47, 58–60
Mystical Body of Christ, 36–44, 46–47, 60, 66, 69, 96, 182
    ecclesiology of, 29, 57, 85
    Vatican II, importance to, 55, 95
Mystici Corporis Christi, 29, 37–44, 55–56, 66

N

New Testament, 167–168, 170–171
    the new covenant, 61, 114, 140
    see also specific Books
non-Christians, 64–66, 80–81
    Christian solidarity with, 85–86
    see also modern world
Nostra Aetate, 81

O

ordained ministry, 165
original sin, 27–29, 173

P

pagans, *see* non-Christians
papacy, 41–42, 67–72
    pre-Vatican II, 30–31
    see also Popes
Parakletos, 112–114
Paschal Mystery, 88, 104–107, 135, 142, 172–173
Pastoral Constitution on the Church in the Modern World, see Gaudium et Spes

Paul, Apostle, Saint, 147, 170–171
    on Christ and the Church, 36–37, 44, 119, 154–156
    on communion and community, 126, 138
    on the Paschal Mystery/ pneumatology, 104–109, 114–115
Paul VI, Pope, 57
peace, 92–93, 181
Peirce, Charles Sanders, 150–151
Pentecost, 46, 68, 110–111
People of God, 60–66, 96, 140–141
"perfect society," Church as, *see societas perfecta*
Peter, Apostle, Saint, 111, 147
    Roman Pontiff as successor, 41, 67–69
pilgrim church, 55, 78
Pius IX, Pope, 34
Pius XII, Pope, 34
    Mystici Corporis Christi, 37–44
pluralism, 81–84
    "interculturation mandate," 64–65
pneuma, 103–115
    see also Holy Spirit; pneumatology
pneumatology, 35–37, 46–50, 95
    and charisms, 119–122
    communion, 124–126
    the pneumatological principle, 166–168
    and spirituality, 117–119
    and the Trinity, 115–117
    universality, principle of, 64–66
    see also Holy Spirit; Paschal Mystery
poets, 138–139
Pontiff, Roman, *see* papacy; Popes
poor, the, 161
Popes
    infallibility of, 71
    Paul VI, *see* Paul VI
    Peter, as successors of, 41, 67–69
    Pius IX, *see* Pius IX
    Pius XII, *see* Pius XII
    see also papacy
prayer, 118, 122, 156–157
preachers, 138–139
presbyterial college, 73
priest(s), priesthood, 62–63, 73
prophet(s)
    in community, 139–140
    Jesus as, 62–64
Protestants
    cooperation with, *see under* Christians

pre-Vatican II attitudes regarding, 30–31, 34–35, 40–41, 45

R

reconciliation, 156–157, 160–161
redemption, 58
Reformation, the, 29, 39
religion(s)
    authentic worship, 112–113
    freedom in, 82–84
    respecting other, 64–65, 81
    see also Christians; non-Christians; spirituality
religious life, 77
resurrection of Jesus, 104–106, 113, 170–172
revelation, 34, 46, 58
rituals, 156–157
Roman Catholic Church, 27–50, 58, 60, 62, 91, 162–166, 174
    Christians, as part of larger body, *see* Body of Christ; Christians; Church of Christ
    Church of Christ and, 143
    as community of communities, 144, 182
    Constitutions on, 53–96, 171–173
    hierarchy in, *see* hierarchy
    laity, *see* laity
    local and universal, 28–29, 69–70, 72, 96, 145
    membership in, 40–41
    mission and role of, *see* mission of the Church
    in the modern world, *see* modern world
    mystery of, 46–47, 58–60
    as "mystical body," *see* Mystical Body of Christ
    as "perfect society," *see* societas perfecta
    pilgrim church, 55, 78
    and Protestants, *see* Christians; Protestants
    universal, *see under* Roman Catholic Church: local and universal (above)
    see also specific topics
Rome, bishop of, 68, 147, 161
Royce, Josiah, 127–138, 144, 160

S

sacrament(s), sacramentality, 55, 59, 66, 97–98, 148–166
    Catholic world view and, 153–156
    Christianity, as fundamental to, 85–86, 153
    Church as sacrament, 47–48, 57, 62, 93, 97–98, 124–125, 153, 155–156, 171
    community and, 153, 157
    of initiation, *see* initiation
    Jesus Christ as, 154–155
    the seven, 156–157
    as signs, 152–153, 157
Sacrosanctum Concilium, 53–96, 158
saints, 78
salvation, 27–30, 43, 79
    the Church and, 65–66, 91, 173–174
    the coming, 78, 89
    God's plan for, 61, 65–66, 81, 89, 171
    grace, as by, *see* grace
    leading others to, 57, 94, 170–171
    see also evangelization
    non-Christians and, 65–66
    the Paschal Mystery, *see* Paschal Mystery
Sapphira, Ananias and, 111
scripture, 58, 158–159
second coming of Christ, 141, 157
servanthood, 139, 158
sharing, *see* charisms; community
sick, anointing of, 156–157
sign(s), 149–153, 160
sin, 171
    original, 27–29, 173
    of selfishness, 111–112, 120
sinners, Church comprised of, 60
societas perfecta, 32–35, 77, 85, 95
Spirit of God, *see* Holy Spirit
spirituality, 117–119
stories, 156–157
storytellers, 138–139
symbol(s), 151–154, 156–158

T

talents, *see* charisms
teachers, 139
    bishops as, 146–147
theologians, prominent, 53–98
    see also individual names
theologies, *see* specific topics
Trent, Council of, 30

Trinity, 46–47, 58, 89–90, 97, 168,
      171–172
      theology of, 115–117
      Vatican II, as central to, 101–102
         see also Holy Spirit; *pneuma;*
            pneumatology
trust, 120, 124
truth, 83, 112–114
Tubingen school, the, 35–37

U

unbelievers, *see* non-Christians
Unitatis Redintegratio, 80–81
unity, 81, 122, 167, 173, 184
      Church and, 40, 63, 65, 80,
         93–94, 146
         see also People of God
         see also community
universality, 64–66
universe, 90–91, 117, 122, 160
      see also creation

V

Vatican I, 30, 33, 37, 57, 71
Vatican II, 182–184
      documents from, major, 53–98
      themes central to, 101–102, 148
         see also communion; Holy Spirit;
            sacrament; Trinity
      theology prior to, 27–50, 181
Virgin Mary, Blessed, 78–80

W

witness, Christian, 63, 122, 125, 140,
      159, 163
      see also evangelization
Word of God, 154, 158–159
      see also scripture
world
      destiny of, 97–98
      modern, *see* modern world
worship, 113, 118